Thomas McArthur Anderson, Army Department United
States, Charles Gauld

Roster of Troops Serving with the Department of the Pacific

and Eighth Army Corps

Thomas McArthur Anderson, Army Department United States, Charles Gauld

Roster of Troops Serving with the Department of the Pacific and Eighth Army Corps

ISBN/EAN: 9783744691680

Printed in Europe, USA, Canada, Australia, Japan

Cover: Foto ©ninafisch / pixelio.de

More available books at **www.hansebooks.com**

ROSTER

OF TROOPS SERVING IN THE

DEPARTMENT OF THE PACIFIC AND EIGHTH ARMY CORPS.

Major General Elwell S. Otis, U. S. Vols.
Brigadier General, U. S. Army,

COMMANDING.

MANILA, PHILIPPINE ISLANDS.

JANUARY, 1899.

ADJUTANT GENERAL'S OFFICE,
HEADQUARTERS DEPARTMENT OF THE PACIFIC
AND EIGHTH ARMY CORPS.

ROSTER

OF TROOPS SERVING IN THE

DEPARTMENT OF THE PACIFIC AND EIGHTH ARMY CORPS.

Major General Elwell S. Otis, U. S. Vols.

Brigadier General, U. S. Army,

COMMANDING.

ANILA, PHILIPPINE ISLANDS.

JANUARY, 1899.

ADJUTANT GENERAL'S OFFICE,
HEADQUARTERS DEPARTMENT OF THE PACIFIC
AND EIGHTH ARMY CORPS.

DEPARTMENT OF THE PACIFIC AND EIGHTH ARMY CORPS.

Major General ELWELL S. OTIS, U. S. Vols.,
Brigadier General, U. S. Army,

COMMANDING.

. ---

PERSONAL STAFF.

Captain C. H. MURRAY, 4th U. S. Cavalry, Aide-de-Camp;

First Lieutenant FRED W. SLADEN, 4th U. S. Infantry, Aide-de Camp. Mustering Officer;

First Lieutenant LOUIS P. SANDERS, 1st Montana Volunteer Infantry, Aide-de-Camp.

DEPARTMENT AND CORPS STAFF.

Lieutenant Colonel THOMAS H. BARRY, U. S. Volunteers, Adjutant General;

Brigadier General R. P. HUGHES, U. S. Volunteers, Inspector General;

Lieutenant Colonel ENOCH H. CROWDER, U. S. Volunteers, Judge Advocate;

Lieutenant Colonel JAMES W. POPE, U. S. Volunteers, Chief Quartermaster;

Colonel DAVID L. BRAINARD, U. S. Volunteers, Chief Commissary;

Lieutenant Colonel HENRY LIPPINCOTT, Deputy Surgeon General, U. S. Army, Chief Surgeon;

Major CHARLES McCLURE, Paymaster, U. S. Army, Chief Paymaster;

Lieutenant Colonel CHARLES L. POTTER, U. S. Volunteers, Chief Engineer Officer;

Captain WILLIAM T. WOOD, 18th U. S. Infantry, Chief Ordnance Officer;

Lieutenant Colonel RICHARD E. THOMPSON, U. S. Volunteers, Chief Signal officer.

ORGANIZATION.

FIRST DIVISION.

MAJOR GENERAL THOMAS M. ANDERSON, U. S. VOLUNTEERS.
Commanding.

Personal Staff.

Second Lieutenant Robert H. Allen, 14th U. S. Infantry, Aide-de-Camp:

Second Lieutenant Thomas M. Anderson, Jr., 13th U. S. Infantry, Aide-de-Camp.

Division Staff.

Captain Henry C. Cabell, A. A. G., U. S. Volunteers, Adjutant General:

Captain William E. Birkhimer, 3d U. S. Artillery, Acting Inspector General and Judge Advocate;

Captain Charles C. Walcutt, A. Q. M., U. S. Volunteers, Chief Quartermaster;

Captain William H. Anderson, C. S., U. S. Volunteers, Chief Commissary;

Major Herbert W. Cardwell, Chief Surgeon, U. S. Volunteers, Chief Surgeon.

Troops Attached to Division Headquarters.

Light Battery D, 6th U. S. Artillery:

Separate Mountain Battery.

1st BRIGADE, 1st DIVISION.

Brigadier General CHARLES KING, U. S. Volunteers,
Commanding.

Personal Staff.

Second Lieutenant Henry M. Merriam, 3d U. S. Artillery, A. D. C.
Second Lieutenant James R. Goodale, 1st New York Volunteer Infantry.
Aide-de-Camp.

Brigade Staff.

Captain Samuel S. Saxton, A. A. G., U. S. Volunteers, Adjutant
General;
Captain Joseph B. Handy, C. S., U. S. Volunteers, Commissary;
Second Lieutenant James A. Hutton, 1st California Volunteer Infantry, Quartermaster.

TROOPS COMPRISING.

Troops C, E, G, I, K and L, 4th U. S. Cavalry;
Headquarters, Band and Companies A, C, D, E, F, G, I, K, L and M,
14th U. S. Infantry;
1st Regiment California Infantry, U. S. Volunteers, (12 companies).

2d BRIGADE, 1st DIVISION.

Brigadier General SAMUEL OVENSHINE, U. S. Volunteers,
Commanding.

Personal Staff.

Second Lieutenant Monroe C. Kerth, 23d U. S. Infantry, A. D. C.

Brigade Staff.

Captain William H. Sage, 23d U. S. Infantry, Acting Adjutant General;
First Lieutenant Frank W. Hunt, 1st Idaho Volunteer Infantry,
Quartermaster;
Major George H. Penrose, Brigade Surgeon, U. S. Volunteers, Surgeon.

TROOPS COMPRISING.

1st Regiment Washington Infantry, U. S. Volunteers, (12 Companies);
1st Regiment Idaho Infantry, U. S. Volunteers, (8 Companies);
1st Regiment North Dakota Infantry, U. S. Volunteers, (8 companies).

SECOND DIVISION.

Major General ARTHUR MacARTHUR, U. S. Volunteers,
Commanding.

Personal Staff.

First Lieutenant Pegram Whitworth 18th U. S. Infantry, Aide-de-Camp.

Division Staff.

Major Putnam Bradlee Strong, A. A. G., U. S. Volunteers, Adjutant
General;

Major John S. Mallory, I. G., U. S. Volunteers, Inspector General;

Captain Charles McClure, 18th U. S. Infantry, Acting Judge Advocate
and Mustering Officer;

Captain Charles G. Sawtelle, Jr., A. Q. M., U. S. Volunteers, Chief
Quartermaster;

Major Robert H. Fitzhugh, C. C. S., U. S. Volunteers, Chief Com
missary;

Major Henry F. Hoyt, Major and Chief Surgeon, U. S. Volunteers.
Chief Surgeon;

Captain C. C. Pierce, Chaplain U. S. Army, Duty with Regular Troops,
Second Division. (Attached).

Troops Attached to Division Headquarters.

Light Batteries A and B, Utah Artillery, U. S. Volunteers.

1st BRIGADE, 2d DIVISION.

BRIGADIER GENERAL H. G. OTIS, U. S. VOLUNTEERS,
Commanding.

Personal Staff.

Second Lieutenant A. W. Bradbury, 7th California Volunteer Infantry,
Aide-de-Camp;

Second Lieutenant P. W. Russell, 1st Nebraska Volunteer Infantry,
Aide-de-Camp and Acting Brigade Quartermaster.

Brigade Staff.

Captain Fred E. Buchan, 20th Kansas Volunteer Infantry, Acting
Adjutant General;

Captain Daniel Van Voorhis, C. S., U. S. Volunteers, Commissary;

Major George F. Shiels, Brigade Surgeon, U. S. Volunteers, Surgeon.

TROOPS COMPRISING.

Batteries G, H, K and L, 3d U. S. Artillery;

1st Regiment Montana Infantry, U. S. Volunteers, (12 Companies);

20th Regiment Kansas Infantry, U. S. Volunteers, (12 Companies);

10th Regiment Pennsylvania Infantry, U. S. Volunteers, (Headquarters
and Companies A, B, C, D, E, H, I and K).

2d BRIGADE, 2d DIVISION.

BRIGADIER GENERAL IRVING HALE, U. S. VOLUNTEERS,
Commanding.

Personal Staff.

Second Lieutenant F. L. Perry, 1st Colorado Volunteer Infantry,
Aide-de-Camp.

Brigade Staff.

Captain A. McD. Brooks, 1st Colorado Volunteer Infantry, Acting
Adjutant General;

First Lieutenant W. B. Sawyer, Q. M., 1st Colorado Volunteer Infantry, Quartermaster;

Captain M. G. Krayenbuhl, C. S., U. S. Volunteers, Commissary;

Major Samuel O. L. Potter, Brigade Surgeon, U. S. Volunteers, Surgeon.

TROOPS COMPRISING.

1st Regiment Colorado Infantry, U. S. Volunteers, (12 Companies);

1st Regiment South Dakota Infantry, U. S. Volunteers, (12 Companies);

1st Regiment Nebraska Infantry, U. S. Volunteers, (12 Companies).

1st SEPARATE BRIGADE.

BRIGADIER GENERAL MARCUS P. MILLER, U. S. VOLUNTEERS,
Commanding.

Personal Staff.

First Lieutenant C. G. Woodward, 3d U. S. Artillery, Aide-de-Camp.

First Lieutenant M. K. Barroll, 3d U. S. Artillery, Aide-de-Camp.

Brigade Staff.

First Lieut. C. G. Woodward, 3d U. S. Artillery, Acting Adjt. Genl.;

Captain Alexander W. Perry, A. Q. M., U. S. Volunteers, Quartermaster;

Captain C. R. Krauthoff, C. S., U. S. Volunteers, Commissary;

Major E. R. Morris, Brigade Surgeon, U. S. Volunteers, Chief Surgeon;

Captain John B. Jeffery, A. Q. M., U. S. Volunteers, Depot Quartermaster at Iloilo; (attached).

Captain Joseph F. Evans, C. S., U. S. Volunteers, (attached).

TROOPS COMPRISING.

Light Battery G, 6th U. S. Artillery;

18th U. S. Infantry, (12 Companies);

51st Regiment Iowa Infantry, U. S. Volunteers, (12 Companies).

PROVOST GUARD.

Brigadier General ROBERT P. HUGHES, U. S. Volunteers,
Commanding.

Personal Staff.

First Lieutenant C. W. Lothrop, 1st Colorado Volunteer Infantry, Aide-de-Camp, In charge of License Bureau:

First Lieutenant C. A. Clark, 13th Minnesota Volunteer Infantry, Aide-de-Camp.

Staff.

Brigadier General C. McC. Reeve, U. S. Volunteers, Deputy Provost Marshal, Chief of Police City of Manila;

Major C. H. Potter, 14th U. S. Infantry, Acting Adjutant General:

Major T. D. Kelcher, Additional Paymaster, U. S. Volunteers, Disbursing Officer;

Major F. S. Bourns, Chief Surgeon, U. S. Volunteers, President Board of Health:

Captain Charles H. Martin, A. Q. M, U. S. Volunteers, Quartermaster:

First Lieutenant R. Platt, 2d Oregon Volunteer Infantry, Acting Judge Advocate;

Captain T. R. Hamer, 1st Idaho Volunteer Infantry. Judge Inferior Provost Court:

Captain L. Feliger, 23d U. S. Infantry. In charge Department of Sanitation:

Captain W. P. Moffett, 1st North Dakota Volunteer Infantry, In charge of Records of Prisons:

Captain W. D. McKinnon, Chaplain 1st California Volunteer Infantry, In charge of Schools, Cemeteries, and Burial Permits:

First Lieutenant H. D. Lackore, 13th Minnesota Volunteer Infantry. In charge of Illumination of Streets and Public Buildings:

Second Lieutenant W. D. Connor, Corps of Engineers, U. S. A., In charge of Water Supply.

Acting Assistant Surgeon C. McQuesten, U. S. Army, Member Board of Health:

Acting Assistant Surgeon B. Ffoulkes, U. S. Army, Member Board of Health:

First Lieutenant W. A. Alexander, 1st Tennessee Volunteer Infantry, Duty in connection with Water Supply.

TROOPS COMPRISING.

23rd U. S. Infantry, (12 Companies):

2d Regiment Oregon Infantry, U. S. Volunteers, (12 Companies):

13th Regiment Minnesota Infantry. U. S. Volunteers, (12 Companies):

1st Regiment Tennessee Infantry, U. S. Volunteers, (8 Companies).

DISTRICT OF CAVITE, P. I.

COLONEL WILLIAM C. SMITH, 1st TENNESSEE VOL. INFANTRY,
Commanding.

District Staff.

First Lieutenant J. K. Polk, 1st Tennessee Volunteer Infantry, Acting
Adjutant General;

Second Lieutenant P. L. Stacker, 1st Tennessee Volunteer Infantry,
Quartermaster;

Captain P. L. Jones, Assistant Surgeon, 1st Tennessee Volunteer
Infantry, Surgeon;

Captain S. M. Milliken, C. S., U. S. Volunteers, Depot Commissary;

TROOPS COMPRISING.

1st Regiment Tennessee Infantry, U. S. Volunteers, (Headquarters
and Companies B, D, L and M;

1st Battalion Wyoming Infantry, U. S. Volunteers, (Companies C, F,
G and H;

Batteries A and D, California Heavy Artillery, U. S. Volunteers;

Light Battery A, Wyoming Artillery, U. S. Volunteers;

Troop A, Nevada Cavalry, U. S. Volunteers.

ATTACHED TO EIGHTH ARMY CORPS.

1st and 18th Companies Signal Corps, U. S. ~~Army.~~ *Vols*

LIEUTENANT COLONEL RICHARD E. THOMPSON, U. S. VOLUNTEERS,
Commanding.

Company A, Engineer Battalion, U. S. ~~Volunteers~~ *Army*

FIRST LIEUTENANT W. G. HAAN, 3D U. S. ARTILLERY,
Commanding.

UNDER ORDERS TO JOIN.

3d U. S. Infantry;
4th U. S. Infantry;
12th U. S. Infantry;
17th U. S. Infantry;
20th U. S. Infantry;
22d U. S. Infantry.

Troops in Department.

ORGANIZATION	GENERAL OFFICERS	STAFF OFFICERS	N. C. Officers, General Staff	INFANTRY Officers	INFANTRY Enlisted Men	CAVALRY Officers	CAVALRY Enlisted Men	ARTILLERY Officers	ARTILLERY Enlisted Men	ENGINEERS Officers	ENGINEERS Enlisted Men	SIGNAL CORPS Officers	SIGNAL CORPS Enlisted Men	MEDICAL DEP'T AND HOSPITAL CORPS Officers	MEDICAL DEP'T AND HOSPITAL CORPS Enlisted Men	TOTAL Officers	TOTAL Enlisted Men
Department and Corps Staff	1	21	8			1		5	129	3		1		1		33	
1st Division	3	6		171	4610	8	581	21	1632							195	5570
2nd Division	3	8		259	5910			7	139							291	6649
1st Separate Brigade	1	4		77	2084											80	2225
Provost Guard	2	2		148	4121											152	4121
District of Cavite		1		34	597	3	88	13	450							51	1135
Signal Corps								1				12	107			12	107
Co. A, Engineer Battalion, U.S.A.										3	115					1	115
Medical Department and Hospital Corps, U.S.A.														*19 16	444	*19 16	444
TOTAL	10	41	8	685	17322	12	619	47	1757	3	115	13	107	*19 16	444	*19 838	20372
Under orders and enroute from the United States	1			†252	17632											†253	17632
GRAND TOTAL	11	41	8	947	20954	12	619	17	1757	3	115	13	107	*19 17	444	*19 1091	28001

* Contract Surgeons   † Estimated maximum strength

GENERAL OFFICERS.

NAME.	RANK.	DUTY.	STA-TIONS.
Otis, E. S.......	Maj. Genl., U. S. Vols..	Military Governor of the Philippine Islands. Comdg. Dept. of the Pacific and 8th Army Corps........	Manila
Anderson, T. M.	Maj. Genl. "	... Commanding 1st Division...... ...	Manila
MacArthur, A...	Maj. Genl. "	...Commanding 2d Division.	Manila
Miller. M. P....	Brig. Genl. "	... Commanding 1st Separate Brigade.....	Iloilo
King, C. ...	Brig. Genl. "	... Commanding 1st Brigade, 1st Division.	Manila
Otis, H. G.	Brig. Genl. . "	...Commanding 1st Brigade, 2d Division.	Manila
Hughes, R. P ...	Brig. Genl. "	...Inspector General, Department Pacific and 8th Army Corps, and Provost Marshal General of Manila.	Manila
Ovenshine, S....	Brig. Genl. "	...Commanding 2d Brigade, 1st Division.	Manila
Hale, I	Brig. Genl. "	...Commanding 2d Brigade, 2d Division.	Manila
Reeve, C. McC..	Brig. Genl. "	...Deputy Provost Marshal General and Chief of Police............... ..	Manila

ADJUTANT GENERAL'S DEPARTMENT.

Barry, Thos. H..	Lieut. Col., A. A. G., U. S. Vols	Adjutant General Department Pacific and 8th Army Corps...	Manila
Strong, P. B. ...	Major, A.A.G., U.S.Vols.	Adjutant General, 2d Division, 8th Army Corps	Manila
Cabell, H. C......	Captain, A. A. G., " ..	Adjutant General, 1st Division, 8th Army Corps...	Manila
Saxton, S. S.. .	Captain, A. A. G., " ...	Adjutant General, 1st Brigade, 1st Division...	Manila

INSPECTOR GENERAL'S DEPARTMENT.

Hughes, R. P....	Brig. Genl, I. G., U. S. Vols	Inspector General, Department Pacific and 8th Army Corps, and Provost Marshal General of Manila.. ...	Manila
Mallory, J. S	Major, I. G., U. S. Vols..	Inspector General, 2d Division..... ...	Manila

JUDGE ADVOCATE'S DEPARTMENT.

Jewett, C. L.....	Lieut. Col., Judge Adv., U. S. Vols.....	....	Enroute to U. S.
Crowder, E. H..	Lieut. Col., Judge Adv., U. S. Vols	Judge Advocate, Department Pacific and 8th Army Corps	Manila

QUARTERMASTER'S DEPARTMENT.

NAME.	RANK.	DUTY.	STATION.
Pope, J. W	Lieut. Col. and C. Q. M., U. S. Vols	Chief Quartermaster, Department of Pacific and 8th Army Corps	Manila
Jones, S. R	Major and Q. M., U. S. Vols	Depot Quartermaster, Binondo	Manila
Devol, C. A.	Major and Q. M., U. S. Vols	Assistant to Chief Quartermaster. In charge of Land and Water Transportation	Manila
Walcutt, C. C.	Captain and A. Q. M., U. S. Vols.	Chief Quartermaster, 1st Division	Manila
Jeffery, J. B.	Captain and A. Q. M., U. S. Vols	Depot Quartermaster	Iloilo
Kimball, A. W.	Captain and A. Q. M., U. S. Vols	Assistant to Chief Quartermaster. In charge of Artillery and Cavalry Stables and Conveyances for command	Manila
Sawtelle, C. G.	Captain and A. Q. M., U. S. Vols	Chief Quartermaster, 2d Division	Manila
Perry, A. W.	Captain and A. Q. M., U. S. Vols	Quartermaster, 1st Separate Brigade	Iloilo
Sulzer, R.	Captain and A. Q. M., U. S. Vols.	Assistant to Chief Quartermaster	Manila
Bradley, J. J	Captain and A. Q. M., U. S. Vols	A. Q. M. and A. C. S., Steamer Arizona.	Manila
Martin, C. H.	Captain and A. Q. M., U. S. Vols	Quartermaster, Provost Guard	Manila

POST QUARTERMASTER SERGEANTS.

NAME.	DUTY.	STATION.
Neisser, S. M.	Duty in Office Depot Quartermaster	Manila

SUBSISTENCE DEPARTMENT.

NAME.	RANK.	DUTY.	STATION.
Brainard, D. L.	Colonel, C.C.S., U. S.Vols	Chief Commissary, Department Pacific and 8th Army Corps	Manila
Cloman, S. A	Major, C. S.	Depot Commissary, Binondo. Purchasing Commissary, Manila and vicinity	Manila
Fitzhugh, R. H.	Major, C. C. S.	Chief Commissary, 2d Division	Manila
Van Voorhis, D.	Captain, C. S., "	Commissary, 1st Brigade, 2d Division.	Manila
Bootes, S. B	Captain, C. S., "	In charge of issues to Spanish prisoners	Manila
Milliken, S. M.	Captain, C. S., "	Depot Commissary, Cavite	Cavite
Anderson, W. H.	Captain, C. S., "	Chief Commissary, 1st Division, and in charge of issues to the command.	Manila

SUBSISTENCE DEPARTMENT.—Continued.

NAME.	RANK.	DUTY.	STA-TION.
Handy, J. B.	Captain, C. S.,U. S. Vols	Commissary, 1st Brigade, 1st Division.	Manila
Coudert, C. du P.	Captain, C. S., "	Assistant to Chief Commissary, In charge of Commissary Sales Depot, Ermita	Manila
Evans, J. F	Captain, C. S., "	With 1st Separate Brigade	Iloilo
Krayenbuhl,M.G	Captain, C. S., "	Commissary, 2d Brigade, 2d Division. In charge Commissary Sales Depot, Quiapo	Manila
Krauthoff, C. R	Captain, C. S., "	Commissary, 1st Separate Brigade	Iloilo

COMMISSARY SERGEANTS.

NAME.	DUTY.	STATION.
Lynch, Patrick	Duty in Office of Assistant to Chief Commissary	Manila
McCaffery, Francis	Duty in Office Depot Commissary, Binondo.	Manila
Zimmerman, C. F. B	Duty in Office Depot Commissary, Binondo	Manila
O'Reilly, Garret	Duty in Office Depot Commissary, Binondo	Manila
Wilson, Henry	Sick in Hospital	Manila
Castle, George P	Duty with Commissary, 1st Separate Brigade	Iloilo
Mausie, William	Duty in Office Depot Commissary, Cavite	Cavite

MEDICAL DEPARTMENT.

NAME.	RANK.	DUTY.	STA-TION.
Lippincott, H	Lieut. Col. Dep. Sur. Genl., U. S. Army	Chief Surgeon, Department of the Pacific and 8th Army Corps	Manila
Corbusier, W. H.	Major and Surgeon, U.S. Army	Medical Supply Depot	Manila
Cardwell, H. W.	Major, Chief Surgeon, U. S. Vols	Chief Surgeon, 1st Division.	Manila
Hoyt, H. F	Major, Chief Surgeon, U. S. Vols	Chief Surgeon, 2d Division	Manila
Bourns, F. S	Major, Chief Surgeon, U. S. Vols	City Health Department	Manila Correg-idor Isl
Owen, W. O.	Major, Brigade Surgeon, U. S. Vols	Convalescent Hospital, Corregidor Isl.	idor Isl
Crosby, Wm. D.	Major, Brigade Surgeon, U. S. Vols	In Charge 1st Reserve Hospital	Manila
Morris, E. R.	Major, Brigade Surgeon, U. S. Vols	Chief Surgeon, 1st Separate Brigade	Iloilo Enroute
Woodruff, C. E.	Major, Brigade Surgeon, U. S. Vols	Detached Service	To U. S. Scandia.
Potter, S. O. L.	Major, Brigade Surgeon, U. S. Vols	Brigade Surgeon, 2d Brigade, 2d Division, and Attending Surgeon, Hdqrs. Dept. Pac.	Manila
Penrose, Geo. H.	Major, Brigade Surgeon, U. S. Vols	Brigade Surgeon, 2d Brigade, 1st Division, and Attending Surgeon, 1st Reserve Hospital	Manila
Shiels, G. F	Major, Brigade Surgeon, U. S. Vols	Brigade Surgeon, 1st Brigade, 2d Division	Manila
Cabell, J. M	Captain, (retired).	Assistant to Chief Surgeon, Dept. Pac. and Eighth Army Corps	Malate
McVay, H. E.	Captain, Asst. Surgeon, U. S. Army	In charge Bacteriological Laboratory	Died Jan. 4
Keefer, F. R.	Captain, Asst. Surgeon, U. S. Army	In charge 2d Reserve Hospital	Malate
Straub, P. F	Captain, Asst. Surgeon, U. S. Army	Asst. Surgeon, 1st Reserve Hospital	Manila
Kemp, F. M.	1st Lieut. Asst. Surgeon, U. S. Army	Surgeon, 14th U. S. Infantry	Malate

MEDICAL DEPARTMENT--Continued.

NAME.	RANK.	DUTY.	STA-TION.
Clayton, J. B	1st Lieut, Asst. Surgeon, U. S. Army	Surgeon, District Hospital.	Cavite
Page, Henry	1st Lieut, Asst. Surgeon, U. S. Army	Asst. Surgeon, Convalescent Hospital.	Correg-idor Isl
Richardson, G.H	Acting Asst. Surgeon, U. S. Army	Asst. Surg., 1st Reserve Hospital.	Manila
Johnstone, E. K.	Acting Asst. Surgeon, U. S. Army	Asst. Surg., Convalescent Hospital	Correg-idor Isl
Mathews, G. W.	Acting Asst. Surgeon, U. S. Army	Surgeon, 3d U. S. Artillery.	Manila
Titus, F. H	Acting Asst. Surgeon, U. S. Army	Asst. Surg., District Hospital	Cavite
Daywalt, G. W	Acting Asst. Surgeon, U. S. Army	Temporary duty with 1st Idaho Vol. Infantry	Manila
McQuesten, C.	Acting Asst. Surgeon, U. S. Army	City Health Department	Manila
Kellogg, P. S.	Acting Asst. Surgeon, U. S. Army	Surgeon Utah Light Artillery	Manila
Walker, M. M.	Acting Asst. Surgeon, U. S. Army	Surgeon 4th U. S. Cavalry	Paco Dist.
Quinan, C	Acting Asst. Surgeon, U. S. Army	Surgeon Bat. D, 6th U. S. Artillery	Manila
Phelan, H. duR.	Acting Asst. Surgeon, U. S. Army	Surgeon Bat. G, 6th U. S. Artillery	Iloilo
de May, C. F	Acting Asst. Surgeon, U. S. Army	Asst. Surg, 2d Oregon Vol. Infantry	Manila
Taylor, W. O.	Acting Asst. Surgeon, U. S. Army	Asst. Surg., District Hospital	Cavite
Bartlett, C. J.	Acting Asst. Surgeon, U. S. Army	Asst. Surg., 2d Reserve Hospital.	Malate
Ffoulkes, B.	Acting Asst. Surgeon, U. S. Army	City Health Department	Manila
Ladd, I. B.	Acting Asst. Surgeon, U. S. Army	Surgeon, 23d U. S. Infantry	Manila
Beasley, S. O	Acting Asst. Surgeon, U. S. Army	Asst. Surg., 2d Reserve Hospital..	Manila
Huntington, S. D	Acting Asst. Surgeon, U. S. Army	Asst. Surg., 1st Reserve Hospital.	Manila
Christensen, W.A	Acting Asst. Surgeon, U. S. Army	Asst. Surg., 23d U. S. Infantry.	Manila
Gunn, H	Acting Asst. Surgeon, U. S. Army	Asst. Surgeon, 18th U. S. Infantry	Iloilo
McCarthy, W. D.	Major and Surgeon, 1st Cal. Vol. Inf	Regimental Surgeon	Manila
Barr, R. A	Major and Surgeon, 1st Tenn. Vol. Inf	Regimental Surgeon	Manila
Snyder, F. A.	Major and Surgeon, 1st Neb. Vol. Inf	Regimental Surgeon	Manila
Adams, F. J.	Major and Surgeon, 1st Mont. Vol. Inf	Regimental Surgeon.	Manila
Fitzgerald, R. J.	Major and Surgeon, 13th Minn. Vol. Inf..	Operator, 1st Reserve Hospital	Manila
Neff, G. N	Major and Surgeon, 10th Penn. Vol. Inf.	Regimental Surgeon	Manila
Mathews, W.H. S	Major and Surgeon, 51st Iowa Vol. Inf.	Detached Service	S. F.
Springer, W. D.	Major and Surgeon, 1st Idaho Vol. Inf	Regimental Surgeon	Manila
Ellis, M. H	Major and Surgeon, 2d Oregon Vol Inf	Regimental Surgeon	Manila
Rafter, J. A	Major and Surgeon, 20th Kansas Vol. Inf.	Regimental Surgeon	Manila
Pease, F. D	Major and Surgeon, 1st N. Dakota Vol. Inf.,	Regimental Surgeon	Manila
Warne, R. C.	Major and Surgeon, 1st S. Dakota Vol. Inf.	Regimental Surgeon	Manila
Kemble, L. H.	Major and Surgeon, 1st Col. Vol. Inf	Regimental Surgeon	Manila

MEDICAL DEPARTMENT.---Continued.

NAME.	RANK.	DUTY.	STA-TION.
Dawson, L. R....	Major and Surgeon, 1st Wash. Vol. Inf	Regimental Surgeon	Manila
Locke, C. E......	Captain and Asst. Surg., 1st Col. Vol. Inf	Asst. Surg., 1st Reserve Hospital	Manila
Farrell, P. J. H .	Captain and Asst. Surg., 1st Cal. Vol. Inf.	On duty with Regiment	Manila
Kirby-Smith,RM	Captain and Asst. Surg., 1st Tenn. Vol. Inf	On duty with Regiment	Manila
Mullins, C. L...	Captain and Asst. Surg., 1st Neb. Vol. Inf	On duty S. S. Ohio	Enroute to U. S.
Law, A. A......	Captain and Asst. Surg., 13th Minn. Vol. Inf.	Regimental Surgeon	Manila
Van Patten,W.M	Captain and Asst. Surg., 1st Wash. Vol. Inf.	On duty with Regiment	Manila
Whiting, S......	Captain and Asst. Surg., 2d Oregon Vol. Inf.	In charge Small-pox Hospital	Manila
Huffman, C. H..	Captain and Asst. Surg., 20th Kansas Vol. Inf	Surgeon, 18th U. S. Infantry	Iloilo
Smith, H. D....	Captain and Asst. Surg., 20th Kansas Vol. Inf	On duty with Regiment	Manila
Jones, P. L.....	Captain and Asst. Surg., 1st Tenn. Vol. Inf...	On duty with Regiment	Cavite
Black, N. M.....	Captain and Asst. Surg., 1st N. Dak. Vol. Inf.	Asst. Surg., 1st Reserve Hospital	Manila
Bowman, A. H..	Captain and Asst. Surg., 1st S. Dak. Vol. Inf..	On duty with Regiment	Manila
Cox, F. W. ...	Captain and Asst. Surg., 1st S. Dak. Vol. Inf .	On duty with Regiment	Manila
O'Brien, A P....	Captain and Asst. Surg., 1st Cal. Vol. Inf.....	On duty S. S. Senator	Enroute to U. S.
Hanna, W. F ..	Captain and Asst. Surg., 1st Cal. Heavy Art..	Regimental Surgeon	Cavite
Morrison, J. F ..	1st Lieut, Asst. Surgeon, 1st Wyoming V. Inf.	Regimental Surgeon	Manila
Jensen, R. P. ...	1st Lieut, Asst. Surgeon, 1st Neb. Vol. Inf ..	On duty with Regiment	Manila
Coffin, J. W....	1st Lieut, Asst. Surgeon, 10th Penn. Vol. Inf .	On duty with Regiment	Manila
McCormick, L. P.	1st Lieut, Asst. Surgeon, 10th Penn. Vol. Inf..	Asst. Surg., 1st Reserve Hospital	Manila
Bruning, L. C..	1st Lieut, Asst. Surgeon, 1st Mont. Vol. Inf.	On duty with Regiment	Manila
Fairchild, D.S.Jr	1st Lieut, Asst. Surgeon, 51st Iowa Vol. Inf...	Regimental Surgeon	Iloilo
MacRay, D. Jr, .	1st Lieut, Asst. Surgeon, 51st Iowa Vol. Inf...	On duty with Regiment	Iloilo
Ritchie, H. P...	1st Lieut, Asst. Surgeon, 13th Minn. Vol. Inf.	On duty with Regiment	Manila
Southmayd, L.	1st Lieut, Asst. Surgeon, 1st Mont. Vol. Inf. .	Asst. Surg., 2d Reserve Hospital	Manila
Conant, J. L. ...	1st Lieut, Asst. Surgeon, 1st Idaho Vol. Inf...	Asst. Surg., 1st Reserve Hospital	Manila
Thornton, D. D..	1st Lieut, Asst. Surgeon, 1st Col. Vol. Inf.....	On duty with Regiment	Manila
Brown, E. M	1st Lieut, Asst. Surgeon, 1st Wash. Vol. Inf ..	On duty with Regiment	Manila

HOSPITAL STEWARDS.

NAME.	RANK.	STATION.
Kuch, Herman	Special duty, Chief Surgeon's Office	Manila
Von Radesky, Charles	Special duty, Medical Supply Depot	Manila
Gerathy, Robert F	Convalescent Hospital	Correg 1st.
Wagnitz, Edward J.	Special duty, Chief Surgeon's Office	Manila
Klar, Frank	Chief Surgeon's Office, 1st Separate Brigade	Iloilo
Gieseking, Fred	1st Reserve Hospital	Manila
Dene, Monckton	2d Reserve Hospital	Malate
Hare, Thomas D	On furlough to January 10, 1899	
Cox, Shelby S	Convalescent Hospital	Correg. 1st.
Jackson, Howard R.	1st Reserve Hospital	Manila
Hoch, Hans	Duty with 18th Infantry	Iloilo

PAY DEPARTMENT.

NAME.	RANK.	DUTY.	STATION.
McClure, Chas.	Major, P. M., U. S. Army	Chief Paymaster, Department Pacific and 8th Army Corps	Manila
Kilbourne, C. E.	Major, P. M., "	Treasurer and Custodian of Public Funds	Manila
Gambrill, Wm. G	Major, Add. P. M., U S. Vols	Paymaster, Department Pacific and 8th Army Corps	Manila
Fitzgerald, H. C.	Major, Add. P. M., U. S. Vols	Paymaster, Department Pacific and 8th Army Corps	Manila
Keleher, T. D.	Major, Add. P. M., U. S. Vols	Disbursing duty in office of Provost Marshal General of Manila	Manila
Rochester,W.B.Jr	Major, Add. P. M., U. S. Vols	Paymaster, Department Pacific and 8th Army Corps	Manila
Schofield, W. B.	Major, Add. P. M., U. S. Vols	Paymaster, Department Pacific and 8th Army Corps	Manila
Sears, John M.	Major, Add. P. M., U. S. Vols	Paymaster, Department Pacific and 8th Army Corps	Manila
Sheary, M. F.	Major, Add. P. M., U. S. Vols	Paymaster, Department Pacific and 8th Army Corps	Manila
Sternberg, T.	Major, Add. P. M., U. S. Vols	Paymaster, Department Pacific and 8th Army Corps	Manila

CORPS OF ENGINEERS.

Potter, C. L.	Lieut. Col., U. S. Vols.	Chief Engineer Officer, Department of the Pacific and 8th Army Corps	Manila
Bell, J. F.	Major, "	In Charge Bureau of Military Information	Manila
Haan, W. G.	1st Lieut., 3d U. S. Art.	Commanding Company A, Battalion of Engineers	Manila
Connor, W. D.	2d Lieut., U. S. Eng. Corps	In charge of City Water Works	Manila

SIGNAL CORPS, U. S. VOLS.

NAME.	RANK.	DUTY.	STATION.
Thompson, R. E	Lieut. Colonel	Chief Signal Officer, Department of the Pacific and 8th Army Corps	Manila
Bailey, W. O	2d Lieutenant	Office Chief Signal Officer, Department of the Pacific and 8th Army Corps, as Property and Disbursing Officer.	Manila

FIRST COMPANY— No. 6 Calle Aguada.

McKenna, E. A	Captain	Sick in Hospital	Manila
Lawrence, G. E	Captain	Special duty in connection with preparation of War Dept. series of photographs	Manila
Tilly, Geo. H	1st Lieutenant	With 1st Separate Brigade	Iloilo
Perkins, P. J	1st Lieutenant	Sick in Hospital	Manila
Rudd, Alson J	2d Lieutenant	Sick in Hospital	Manila
Chance, Wm. W	1st Lieutenant, 11th Co.	Sick in Hospital	Manila

EIGHTEENTH COMPANY—No. 2 Calle Aguada.

Nesmith, O. A	Captain	Office Chief Signal Officer of Army	Wash. D. C.
Russel, Edgar	Captain	Commanding company; in charge of Military Telephone System	Manila
Bailey, F. H	1st Lieutenant	With company	Manila
Kilbourne, C. E. Jr	1st Lieutenant	Commanding 1st company	Manila
Gordon, C. H	2d Lieutenant	With company	Manila
Cannon, W. C	2d Lieutenant	With 1st Separate Brigade	Iloilo

Fourth U. S. Cavalry.

TROOPS AND ADDRESS.	OFFICERS.	RANK.	DUTY.
Headquarters. Exposition Grounds, Paco.	Rucker, Louis H	Major	Commanding squadrons
Troop C Exposition Grounds, Paco.	Gale, George H. G.	Captain	Commanding troop
	Winans, Edwin B., jr	1st Lieutenant	Unknown
	Carson, Thomas G	2d Lieutenant	Commanding troop K
Troop E Exposition Grounds, Paco.	Wheeler, Fred	Captain	Commanding troop
	Batson, Matthew A	1st Lieutenant	A. D. C. to Major General Wheeler
	Eltinge, LeRoy	2d Lieutenant	Commanding troop G
Troop G Exposition Grounds, Paco.	McGrath, Hugh J	Captain	Major of Engineers U. S. Vols.
	Brown, Robert A	1st Lieutenant	Major and A. I. G. U. S. Vols.
	Parker, James S	2d Lieutenant	Commanding troop L
Troop I Exposition Grounds, Paco.	Lockett, James	Captain	Commanding troop
	Cameron, George H.	1st Lieutenant	Unknown
	Boyd, Charles T	2d Lieutenant	Squadron Adjutant. A. A. Q. M. and A. C. S.
Troop K Exposition Grounds, Paco.	Benson, Harry C	Captain	Major and A. I. G. U. S. Vols.
	Scherer, Louis C	1st Lieutenant	On D. S. at Mount Gretna, Pa.
	Rutherford, Sam'l. McP.	2d Lieutenant	U. S. Infantry and Cavalry School
Troop L Exposition Grounds, Paco.	Murray, Cunliffe H.	Captain	Aide-de-Camp to Major General E. S. Otis
	O'Shea, John	1st Lieutenant	
	Cossatt, Edward B	2d Lieutenant	On D. S. on transport "Tacoma" On D. S. at Tampa, Fla.

Nevada Volunteer Cavalry.

TROOPS AND ADDRESS.	OFFICERS.	RANK.	DUTY.
Troop A Corner Calle Arsenal and Calle Telegrafo, Cavite.	Linscott, Fred M	Captain	Commanding troop
	Gignoux, Frederick E.	1st Lieutenant	With troop
	Wright, Walter O	2d Lieutenant	" "

Third U. S. Artillery.

BATTERIES AND ADDRESS.	OFFICERS.	RANK.	DUTY.
Headquarters... Cuartel de Meisie, Tondo.	Kobbe, William A	Major	Commanding battalions.
Battery G. ...... Cuartel de Meisie, Tondo.	Randolph, Benjamin H.	Captain.	Commanding battery
	Wilson, Eugene T	1st Lieutenant... ..	D. S. at San Francisco.
	Overton, Winfield S . .	2d Lieutenant ...	On leave
	James, Harry L.	2d Lieutenant	On leave
Battery H. .... Cuartel de Meisie, Tondo.	O'Hara, James	Captain	Commanding 1st battalion
	Barroll, Morris K	1st Lieutenant.....	Aid to Brig. Gen. Miller
	Kessler, Percy M..	2d Lieutenant . .	Adjt. and Cm'dg. battery.
	Boutelle, Henry. M....	2d Lieutenant	With battery
Battery K .... Cuartel de Meisie, Tondo.	Hobbs, Charles W	Captain	Commanding 2d battalion
	Krayenbuhl, Maurice G.	1st Lieut., Captain and C. S.,U. S.Vols	Com'sy, 2d Brig., 2d Div.
	England, Lloyd	2d Lieutenant	Commanding battery
	Lanza, Conrad H.... ..	2d Lieutenant......	With battery
Battery L ...... Cuartel de Meisie, Tondo.	Birkhimer, William E..	Captain	A. I. G. 1st Division
	Haan, William G........	1st Lieutenant......	Commanding company A, Battalion of Engineers
	Abernethy, Robert S....	2d Lieutenant	Commanding battery H. A. A. Q. M. and A. C. S...
	Kimmel, Edward	2d Lieutenant	With battery

Light Batteries 6th U. S. Artillery.

Battery D .... .. Pavilion de Luneta, East of Walled City.	Dyer, Alexander B.....	Captain...	Commanding battery
	Hawthorne, Harry L....	1st Lieutenant......	Commanding Separate Mountain Battery
	Fleming, Adrian S:....	2d Lieutenant	With battery
	Scott, E. D	2d Lieutenant	" "
	Koehler, R. M	2d Lieutenant	" Separate Mountain Battery
Battery G...:.... Iollo	Bridgman, Victor H....	Captain....	Commanding battery
	Ostheim, Louis	1st Lieutenant......	With battery
	Pearce, Earle D'A	2d Lieutenant	" "
	Pearce, Fred A.........	2d Lieutenant	" "
	Babcock, Conrad S	2d Lieutenant.......	" "

Separate Mountain Battery.

Pavilion de Luneta, East of Walled City.	Hawthorne, H. L.......	1st Lieutenant......	Commanding battery
	Koehler, R. M..........	2d Lieutenant......	With battery

California Volunteer Heavy Artillery.

Batteries and Address.	Officers.	Rank.	Duty.
Headquarters Calle Novaleiches, Cavite.	Rice, Frank S	Major	Commanding battalion, Provost Marshal, Cavite.
	Koster, John A	1st Lieut. and Adjt.	With battalion
	Hanna, William J	Captain and A. S.	" "
Battery A No. 6 Calle Colon, Cavite.	Geary, Dennis	Captain	Commanding battery and Inspector of Customs, Cavite
	Morse, J. B	1st Lieutenant	With battery
	Hayne, A. P	2d Lieutenant	" "
	Glass, John A	2d Lieutenant	" "
Battery D Cor. Calle Real and Calle Telegrafo, Cavite.	Steere, Henry	Captain	Commanding battery.
	Diss, John W. F	1st Lieutenant	With battery
	McKeeby, George L	2d Lieutenant	" "
	Lucey, John	2d Lieutenant	" "

Utah Volunteer Light Artillery.

Headquarters Cuartel de Meisic, Tondo.	Young, Richard W	Major	Commanding battalion and Acting Judge of Provost Court
Battery A Cuartel de Meisic, Tondo.	Wedgwood, E. A.	Captain	Commanding battery
	Gibbs, George W	1st Lieutenant	Battalion Ord. Officer
	Naylor, Raymond C	2d Lieutenant	With Battery and Battalion Commissary.
	Webb, William C	2d Lieutenant	With Battery and Battalion Adjutant.
Battery B Cuartel de Meisic, Tondo.	Grant, Frank A	Captain	Commanding battery
	Critchlow, John F	1st Lieutenant	With Battery and Bat. Q. M.
	Grow, Orrin R	2d Lieutenant	Sick in hospital
	Seaman, George A	2d Lieutenant	With battery

Wyoming Volunteer Light Artillery.

Battery A Calle Cisneros, Cavite.	Clarke, Harry A	1st Lieutenant	Commanding battery
	Gilmore, James M	2d Lieutenant	With battery

Company A, Battalion of Engineers, U. S. A.

Company A Convent de Malate, Calle Real, Malate.	Haan, William G	1st Lieutenant, 3d U. S. Artillery	Commanding company

Fourteenth U. S. Infantry.

COMPANIES AND ADDRESS.	OFFICERS.	RANK.	DUTY.
Headquarters Field Staff and Band. Cuartel de Malate.	Anderson, Thomas M...	Col.,Maj. Gen. U.S.V.	Commanding 1st Division
	Davis, George W.......	Lieut. Col, Brig. Gen. U. S. Vols......	Com'd'g. 2d Div., 2d Army Corps
	Potter, Carroll H.	Major....	A. A. G., Prov. Mar. Genl's. Headquarters
	(vacancy).............	1st Lieut. and Adjt.	....
	(vacancy).............	1st Lieut and Q. M...	....
	McCain Henry P	1st Lieut. (unassig'd)	Absent, sick.
	Martin, Charles H	1st Lieut. Capt. and A. Q. M.,U. S. V.	Q. M. Provost Guard
	Krauthoff, Charles R ...	1st Lieut., Capt. and C. S., U. S. Vols.	Commissary, 1st Separate Brigade
	Robe, Charles F........	Lt. Col. 17th U. S. I.	Commanding regiment
Company A..... Cuartel de Malate.	Eastman, Frank F......	Captain......	Commanding 3rd battalion
	Lasseigne, Armand I....	1st Lieutenant......	Commanding company D
	(vacancy).............	2d Lieutenant.... ..	....
Company C...... Cuartel de Malate.	Reynolds, William B....	Captain....	Mustr. Officer,State of Kansas
	Biddle, William S. Jr...	1st Lieutenant......	Cm'd'g. company and Acting Regimental Adjt.
	Gohn, Joseph F	2d Lieutenant..... ..	On leave
Company D..... Cuartel de Malate.	McCammon, Wm. W....	Captain	On leave
	Learned, Henry G......	1st Lieutenant	On D.S. in Alaska.
	Field, Robert..........	2d Lieutenant	Commanding Company I
Company E...... Cuartel de Malate.	Taylor, Frank	Captain...........	Mustering Officer, States of Wahington and Oregon.
	Wilhelm, William H. ...	1st Lieutenant......	A. D. C. to Brig. Gen. Snyder
	Miles, Perry L....	2d Lieutenant	Commanding company
Company F...... Cuartel de Malate.	Murphy, John..... ...	Captain..........	Commanding 2d battalion
	Mitchell, James	1st Lieutenant.....	Commanding company
	Wright, Allen G........	2d Lieutenant	In United States
Company G...... Cuartel de Malate.	(vacancy)	Captain...........	....
	Hasbrouck, Alfred Jr...	1st Lieutenant	Commanding company K
	Kemper, James B.......	2d Lieutenant......	On duty with company K.
	Savage, Frank M.......	2d Lieut. 15th Infty.	Commanding company
Company I...... Cuartel de Malate.	Tillson, John C. F......	Captain .. .... 1st Lieut., Capt., A.	Recr. Ser. at Cleveland, O.
	Cabell, Henry C........	A. G., U S. V....	Adjt. Gen. 1st Div.
	Burnside, William A....	2d Lieutenant	Commanding Company L, and Acting Regt'l Q. M.
Company K..... Cuartel de Malate.	Matile, Leon A........	Captain...........	Commanding 1st battalion
	Seay, Samuel Jr.......	1st Lieutenant......	Duty with N. G. Tenn.
	Mullay, Patrick H	2d Lieutenant..... ..	Commanding company M.
Company L...... Cuartel de Malate.	Manning, William L....	Captain	Commanding Jackson Barracks, La.
	(vacancy).............	1st Lieutenant......	....
	Gilbreth, Joseph L.....	2d Lieutenant	Commanding company A.
Company M..... Cuartel de Malate.	Patten, George H.......	Captain...........	Absent, sick
	Bradley, John J........	1st Lieut., Capt. and A. Q. M., U. S. V.	A. Q. M. and A. C. S., S. S. Arizona
	(vacancy)............	2d Lieutenant	.....

Eighteenth U. S. Infantry.

COMPANIES AND ADDRESS.	OFFICERS.	RANK.	DUTY.
Headquarters Field Staff and Band. Iloilo.	Van Valzah, David D.	Colonel	Commanding regiment
	Bailey, Clarence M	Lieut. Colonel	On leave. (Sick)
	Kellar, Chas	Major	Commanding 2d battalion
	Paul, Charles R	Major	Commanding 3d battalion.
	Evans, Frederic D	1st Lieut. and Adjt.	With regiment
	Martin, George W	1st Lieut. and Q. M.	" "
Company A. Iloilo.	Bates, Robert F	Captain	Commanding 1st battalion
	Gordon, Walter H	1st Lieutenant	Colonel Delaware Vol. Inf.
	Jordan, William H	2d Lieutenant	With company
Company B Iloilo.	Griffith, Thomas W	Captain	Commanding company.
	(Vacancy)	1st Lieutenant	
	Conrad, Bryan	2d Lieutenant	With company.
Company C Iloilo.	Warwick, Oliver B	Captain	Commanding company.
	Beall, Fielder M. M.	1st Lieutenant	R. S., San Antonio, Texas.
	Lyle, David E. W	2d Lieutenant	With company.
Company D Iloilo.	Hinton, Charles B	Captain	Commanding company.
	Lewis, Edson A	1st Lieutenant	Commanding Company A.
	Walton, Edward S	2d Lieutenant	Mustering Officer, Springfield Illinois.
	Baldwin, Murray.	1st Lieut. 11th Inf'ty	Attached to company.
Company E Iloilo.	Wheeler, William B	Captain	Commanding company.
	Wells, Briant H	1st Lieutenant	With company.
	Brookes, Albert S	2d Lieutenant	Captain and C. S. U. S. Vol.
	Crimmins, Martin L	2d Lieutenant	With company,
Company F Iloilo.	Hardin, Charles B	Captain	On leave.
	Clark, Elmer W	1st Lieutenant	Commanding company.
	Bolles, Frank C	2d Lieutenant	With company.
Company G Iloilo.	Wood, William T	Captain	Chief Ord. Officer, Dept of Pac. and 8th Army Corps.
	Whitworth, Pegram	1st Lieutenant	A. D. C. to Major General McArthur.
	Fiske, Harold B	2d Lieutenant	Commanding company.
Company H Iloilo.	Steele, Charles L	Captain	On Leave.
	Lowe, Percival G	1st Lieutenant	With Alaska Explor. Exp.
	Grubbs, Hayden Y	2d Lieutenant	Lieut. Col. 2d U. S. Vol. Inf.
	Barnes, John W	2d Lieutenant	Commanding company.
Company I Iloilo.	McClure, Charles	Captain	A. J. A., 2d Division.
	(vacancy)	1st Lieutenant	
	McBroom, Walter S	2d Lieutenant	Commanding company.
Company K Iloilo.	Adams, Henry H	Captain	Recruiting Service, Cincinnati Ohio.
	Hirsch, Harry J	1st Lieutenant	Commanding company.
	Conger, A. L. Jr	2d Lieutenant	With company.
Company L Iloilo.	Hatch, Everard E	Captain	Commanding company.
	Hunt, Ora E.	1st Lieutenant	On leave.
	Falls, Moor N	2d Lieutenant	With company.
Company M Iloilo.	Shanks, David C	Captain	Major Virginia Vol. Inf.
	Grote, William F	1st Lieutenant	Commanding company.
	Aloe Alfred	2d Lieutenant	With company.

Twenty-Third U. S. Infantry.

COMPANIES AND ADDRESS.	OFFICERS.	RANK.	DUTY.
Headquarters Field, Staff and Band. Artillery Barracks, Old Manila.	Ovenshine, Samuel	Colonel, Brig. Gen. U. S. V.	Commanding 1st Brigade, 2d Division.
	French, John W.	Lieut. Colonel	Commanding regiment.
	Spurgin, Wm. F.	Major	West Point, N. Y.
	Goodale, Greenleaf A.	Major	Commanding 1st battalion.
	Hagadorn, Charles B.	1st Lieut. and Adjt.	With regiment
	Cole, Henry G.	1st Lieut. and Q. M.	" "
Company A. Artillery Barracks, Old Manila.	Pendleton, Edwin P.	Captain	Commanding company.
	Thompson, James K.	1st Lieutenant	A. A. G., U. S. Volunteers.
	Goodale, Geo. S.	2d Lieutenant	Commanding company K
Company B. Artillery Barracks, Old Manila.	Cowles, Calvin D.	Captain	Lieut. Colonel, North Carolina Volunteers,
	Stevens, Raymond R.	1st Lieutenant	Commanding company.
	Oury, William H.	2d Lieutenant	With company F.
Company C. Treasury building, Old Manila.	Nichols, William A.	Captain	Commanding company.
	Royden, Herbert N.	1st Lieutenant	Recruiting Service, Providence, R. I.
	Howland, Harry S.	2d Lieutenant	With company M.
Company D. Artillery Barracks, Old Manila.	Febiger, Lea	Captain	Special duty in Office Provost Marshal General; in charge of Dep't. of Sanitation.
	Morse, Benjamin C.	1st Lieutenant	Asst. to Chief Ord. Officer of Dept.
	Hampton, Celwyn E.	2d Lieutenant	Commanding company
Company E. Artillery Barracks, Old Manila.	Pratt, Edward P.	Captain	Commanding 2d battalion
	Edwards, Clarence R.	1st Lieutenant	Asst. Adjt. Genl., U. S. Vols.
	Franklin, Thomas	2d Lieutenant	Commanding company
Company F. Custom House;	Clagett, J. Rozier	Captain	Comdg. company and infy. battalion at Custom House.
	Taylor, John R. M.	1st Lieutenant	Commanding Company L
	Wheeler, David P.	2d Lieutenant	On leave. (Sick)
Company G. Artillery Barracks, Old Manila.	Bolton, Edwin B.	Captain	Commanding 3rd battalion
	Kobbé, Ferdinand W.	1st Lieutenant	Commanding company
	Brambila, Robert M.	2d Lieutenant	Sick in San Francisco, Cal.
Company H. Artillery Barracks, Old Manila.	O'Connor, Stephen	Captain	Commanding company
	Schley, Thomas F.	1st Lieutenant	Commanding company L.
	Lieber, William A.	2d Lieutenant	Sick in quarters.
Company I. Artillery Barracks, Old Manila.	Collins, Charles L.	Captain	Mil. Attache, Caraccas, Ven.
	Devore, Daniel B.	1st Lieutenant	A. A. G., U. S. Vols.
	Macnab, Alexander J.	2d Lieutenant	On duty with company
Company K. Artillery Barracks, Old Manila.	Sage, Wm. H.	Captain	A. A. G., 2d Brig. 1st Div.
	Moore, Geo. D.	1st Lieutenant	On leave
	Conrad, Wm. D.	2d Lieutenant	Sick in hospital
Company L. Artillery Barracks, Old Manila.	Dapray, John A.	Captain	A. G. Dis. Columbia Militia.
	Laubach, Howard T.	1st Lieutenant	Recruiting Ser., Dallas, Tex.
	Kerth, Monroe C.	2d Lieutenant	Aide-de-camp to Brig. Gen'l. Samuel Ovenshine
Company M. Artillery Barracks, Old Manila.	Allaire, William H.	Captain	A. G. Dis. Columbia Militia.
	Stritzinger, F. G. Jr	1st Lieutenant	Commanding company
	Munton, Charles H.	2d Lieutenant	On duty with company C.

First Regiment California Volunteer Infantry.

COMPANIES AND ADDRESS.	OFFICERS.	RANK.	DUTY.
Headquarters Field, Staff, and Band Suspension bridge, west end.	Smith, James F.	Colonel	Commanding regiment
	Duboce, Victor D.	Lieut. Colonel	Commanding 1st battalion
	Tilden, Chas. L.	Major	Sick in San Francisco
	Boxton Chas.	Major.	Commanding 2d battalion
	Sime, Hugh T.	Major	Commanding 3d battalion
	Kelleher, Alfred J.	Captain and Adjt.	With regiment
	Schwerdtfeger, O.	1st Lieut. and Q. M.	With regiment
	West, John J.	1st Lieut., Bat. Adj	With regiment
	Huber, Herman.	1st Lieut., Bat. Adj	With regiment
	Tobin, Wm. H.	1st Lieut., Bat. Adj	Special duty in office of the Provost Marshal General, Department of Sanitation
	Dohrmann, F. W. Jr.	1st Lieutenant	On leave
	McCarthy, Wm. D.	Major and Surgeon.	With regiment
	Farrell, P. J. H.	Captain and As. Sur.	With regiment
	O'Brien, Aloysius P.	Captain and As. Sur.	In charge of sick on S. S. Senator enroute to U. S.
	McKinnon, Wm. D.	Captain, Chaplain	Spe'l. duty, Provost Marshal Gen'l's office, in charge schools cemeteries, burial permits.
Company A Suspension bridge, west end.	Connolly, John F.	Captain	Commanding company
	Ballinger, Geo. T.	1st Lieutenant	With company
	Brown, Joseph A	2d Lieutenant	Temporary duty in P.O. Dep't
Company B Suspension bridge, west end.	Filmer, George.	Captain	Commanding company
	Sturdivant, Benj. B.	1st Lieutenant.	With company
	Ramm, Albert F	2d Lieutenant	" "
Company C Suspension bridge, west end.	Dumbrell, James W	Captain	Commanding company
	Goodell, Chas. E.	1st Lieutenant	With company
	Petty, Geo. J.	2d Lieutenant	Acting battalion Adj't
Company D Suspension bridge, west end.	McCreagh, Thos. J	Captain	Commanding company
	McGurren, Harry F.	1st Lieutenant	With company
	Hutton, James A	2d Lieutenant	Q. M., 1st Brigade, 1st Div.
Company E Suspension bridge, west end.	Robertson, Wm. R	Captain	Commanding company
	Jordan, James H.	1st Lieutenant	In Provost Marshal Genl's. office.
	(Vacancy)	2d Lieutenant.	
Company F Suspension bridge, west end.	Miller, John A	Captain	Commanding company
	Nippert, Firmen A.	1st Lieutenant.	Sick in quarters
	Brown, Frederick L	2d Lieutenant.	With company
Compang G Suspension bridge, west end.	Sutliffe, Edgar C.	Captain	Commanding company
	Sparrowe, Thos. W.	1st Lieutenant	With company
	Swasey, Wm. N.	2d Lieutenant	' '
Company H Suspension bridge, west end.	Warren, Frank W.	Captain	On D. S. at San Francisco
	Davis, Edwin F	1st Lieutenant.	Commanding company
	O'Brien, Timothy P.	2d Lieutenant	With company
Company I Suspension bridge, west end.	(Vacancy).	Captain.	
	Huber, Otto F	1st Lieutenant	Commanding company
	Moore, Frank K	2d Lieutenant	With company
Company K Suspension bridge, west end.	Cunningham, Thos. J	Captain	Commanding company
	Finley, Edward D	1st Lieutenant	With company
	Seely, Carlton W.	2d Lieutenant.	Temporary duty in Post Office Department
Company L Suspension bridge, west end.	Eggert, John F	Captain	Commanding company
	Curzons, Harry E.	1st Lieutenant	With company
	Adler, Albert C.	2d Lieutenant.	" "
Company M Suspension bridge, west end.	O'Neil, Thos. F.	Captain	Commanding company
	Hogan, Chas. J	1st Lieutenant	With company
	Rivers, Edwin W.	2d Lieutenant	" "

First Regiment Colorado Volunteer Infantry.

COMPANIES AND ADDRESS.	OFFICERS	RANK.	DUTY.
Headquarters Field Staff and Band.......... No. 86 Calle Alix.	McCoy, Henry B.......	Colonel	Commanding regiment
	Moses, Cassius M	Lieut. Colonel.....	With regiment .
	Anderson, Charles M....	Major	" "
	Grove, William R.....	Major.............	With regiment
	Kemble, Lewis H	Major and Surgeon..	" "
	Locke, Charles E	Captain and A. S ...	Duty 1st Reserve Hospital
	Thornton, David D . ..	1st Lieut. and A. S..	With regiment
	Fleming, David L......	Captain and Chap...	" "
	Sweeney, Wm. H. Jr...	1st Lieut. and Adjt.	" "
	Sawyer, William B......	1st Lieut. Q. M.....	Q. M. 2d Brigade
Company A.... No. 25 San Sebastian	Stewart, John S.......	Captain	Commanding company
	Doertenbach, Wm. F. ..	1st Lieutenant......	With company
	Thomas Samuel E......	2d Lieutenant	" "
Company B...... No. 46 Calle Alix.	Carroll, Frank M	Captain	Commanding company
	Lewis, Charles B	1st Lieutenant......	With company
	Hooper, Charles E	2d Lieutenant	On leave
Company C. ... No. 12 Plaza de Santa Ana.	Booth, Ewing E.......	Captain	Commanding company
	Means, Rice W........	1st Lieutenant......	With company
	Bidwell, Willard P	2d Lieutenant... ..	" "
Company D.... . No. 1 Calle Alix.	Taylor, John A........	Captain	Commanding company
	Borstadt, George	1st Lieutenant......	Regimental Commissary
	Luther, Albert J........	2d Lieutenant......	With company
Company E...... No. 25 San Sebastian	Rucker, Kyle..........	Captain..........	Commanding company
	Lothrop, Clarence W....	1st Lieutenant......	Charge Bur. of Lic'es, Manila and Aide-de-Camp to Brig. Gen. R. P. Hughes
	Zollars, Charles O.....	2d Lieutenant......	On leave
Company F..... No. 25 San Sebastian	Comings, G. Ralph....	Captain	On leave
	Haughwout, Charles S.	1st Lieutenant.	Asst. to Coll. Internal Rev.
	Riggs, Willard G........	2d Lieutenant	Commanding company
Company G .... Convent San Sebastian.	Howard, David P......	Captain	Commanding company
	Brown, Thomas C	1st Lieutenant......	With company
	Burke, Walter P........	2d Lieutenant......	" "
Company H.... Calle Alix.	Eastman, Charles B.....	Captain..........	Commanding company
	Wilcox, Charles H......	1st Lieutenant......	With company
	Perry, Fred L........	2d Lieutenant......	Aide-de-Camp to Brig. Gen. Irving Hale
Company I...... Convent, San Sebastian.	Brooks, Alexander McD.	Captain	A. A. G. 2d Brig., 2d Div.
	Hilton, Charles H., Jr ..	1st Lieutenant......	Commanding company
	Clotworthy, Henry L....	2d Lieutenant	With company
Company K..... No 12 Plaza de Santa Ana.	Cornell, William A......	Captain......	Sick in quarters
	Vannice, William J	1st Lieutenant······	Sick in quarters
	Lister, Ralph B	2d Lieutenant	Commanding company
Company L ..... No. 20 Calle Alix.	La Salle, David P	Captain	Commanding company
	O'Keefe, Cornelius F....	1st Lieutenant......	Temporary duty, Bur. of Military Information
	Pallou, Franklin, Jr	2d Lieutenant	With company
Company M.... No. 66 Calle Alix.	Spicer, Clyde C.......	Captain	Commanding company
	Sleeper, Charles H......	1st Lieutenant......	Deputy Coll. Inter. Rev.
	Gowdy, James H........	2d Lieutenant	With company

First Regiment Idaho Volunteer Infantry.

COMPANIES AND ADDRESS.	OFFICERS.	RANK.	DUTY.
Headquarters	Jones, John W	Lieut. Colonel	On leave
Field, Staff and	Figgins, Daniel W	Major	Commanding regiment
Band.	McConville, Edward	Major	Commanding battalion
No. 81 Calle Real,	Springer, Warren D	Major and Surgeon	With regiment
Malate.	Conant, Jesse L., Jr.	1st Lieut. and A. S.	Duty at 1st Reserve Hospital.
	Stephenson, Wm. D	Captain and Chap.	With regiment
	Roos, Louis N	1st Lieut. and Ad'jt.	" "
	Graham, James	1st Lieut. and Q. M.	" "
Company A	McRoberts, Phil W	Captain	Commanding company
Calle Real, opposite	Syms, Henry J	1st Lieutenant	With company
Cuartel de Malate.	Steunenberg, George E	2d Lieutenant	" "
Company B	Schattner, Louis D	Captain	Commanding company
Exposition Building,	Martinson, Edward O	1st Lieutenant	With company and Bat. Ad, t
Ermita.	Barbour, John O	2d Lieutenant	On leave
Company C	Murphy, John W	Captain	On leave
Exposition Building,	Hartman, Richard H	1st Lieutenant	Commanding company
Ermita.	Holden, Edwin M	2d Lieutenant	With company
Company D	Smith, Edward	Captain	Commanding company
Exposition Building,	Gage, Wells E.	1st Lieutenant	With company
Ermita.	Bell, James K	2d Lieutenant	" "
Company E	Hamer, Thomas R	Captain	Judge of Inferior Provost Court
Calle Real, opposite	Castle, Levi	1st Lieutenant	Commanding company
Cuartel de Malate.	York, Frank G	2d Lieutenant	With company
Company F	Linck, Max J	Captain	Commanding 1st Battalion
No. 25 and 74, Calle	Kipp, William J	1st Lieutenant	Commanding company
Real, Paco.	Busby, L. M.	2d Lieutenant	With company and Bat. Adj't.
Company G	Whittington, Wm. E	Captain	Commanding company
Exposition Building,	Hunt, Frank W	1st Lieutenant	Q. M. 1st Brigade, 2d Div.
Ermita.	Tschudy, Robert H	2d Lieutenant	Acting Ord. Officer
Company H	Fenn, Frank A	Captain	Commanding company
No 74 Nozaleda,	Worthman Harry S	1st Lieutenant	With company
Paco.	Hawley, Edgar T	2d Lieutenant	" "

Fifty-first Regiment Iowa Volunteer Infantry.

COMPANIES AND ADDRESS.	OFFICERS	RANK.	DUTY.
Headquarters Field, Staff and Band ...... Iloilo.	Loper, John C.	Colonel	Commanding regiment
	Miller, Marcellus M.	Lieut. Colonel.....	With regiment
	Duggan, William J...	Major	" "
	Hume, John T.........	Major..............	" "
	Moore, Sterling P....	Major..........	" "
	Mathews, Willard S. H.	Major and Surgeon..	At San Francisco
	Macrae, Donald Jr.....	1st Lieut. and A. S.	With regiment
	Fairchild, David S. Jr..	1st Lieut. and A. S.	" "
	Williams, Hermon P....	Captain and Chap..	" "
	Davidson, Joseph T....	Captain and Adj't...	" "
	Cady, John D.	1st Lieut. and Q. M.	" "
	Reed, George A.	1st Lieut. Bat. Adj.	At San Francisco.
	Compton, Frank M.....	1st Lieut. Bat. Adj.	With regiment
	Lane, Herbert C	1st Lieut. Bat. Adj.	" "
Company A. .... Iloilo.	Gibson, William R....	Captain	Commanding company
	Kihlbom, Frank W.....	1st Lieutenant.....	With company
	Finley, Park A.	2d Lieutenant.....	" "
Company B.... Iloilo.	Burton, Albert F......	Captain	Commanding company
	Baker, James D.... ...	1st Lieutenant	With company
	Scholz, Samuel B.	2d Lieutenant	" "
Company C...... Iloilo.	Steepy, William F.....	Captain	Sick in hospital
	Dull, Harry B.	1st Lieutenant.....	Commanding company
	Wilson George W......	2d Lieutenant.	With company
Company D.... Iloilo.	Butterfield, Louis K....	Captain	Commanding company
	Hoover, Miles R	1st Lieutenant	Sick in hospital
	Mentzer, William C.....	2d Lieutenant	With company
Company E...... Iloilo.	Mount, Charles V......	Captain	Commanding company
	Ross, James O.	1st Lieutenant	With company
	Williams, Lemont A....	2d Lieutenant	" "
Company F...... Iloilo.	Keating, William H..	Captain	Commanding company
	Point, Will H	1st Lieutenant......	With company
	Hearne, Edward W.....	2d Lieutenant.....	" "
Company G...... Iloilo.	Ickis, Warren H........	Captain	Commanding company
	Ohlschlager, William F.	1st Lieutenant.....	With company
	Edaburn, James	2d Lieutenant	" "
Company H..... Iloilo.	Worthington, Emery C	Captain	Commanding company
	Bennett, Earnest R ...	1st Lieutenant	With company
	Baker, Fred L........	2d Lieutenant	" "
Company I...... Iloilo.	Widner, William B.....	Captain	Commanding company
	Gaines, Richard J.......	1st Lieutenant.....	With company
	Fuller, Rennie H.	2d Lieutenant	" "
Company K . Iloilo.	Peairs, Emerson C......	Captain	Commanding company
	Mitchell, Lenord A.....	1st Lieutenant......	Sick in hospital at Honolulu
	Karnes, Howard G.....	2d Lieutenant	With company
Company L...... Iloilo.	Pryor, Will O.	Captain	Commanding company
	Moore, John L	1st Lieutenant	With company
	Tinley, Matthew A......	2d Lieutenant	" "
Company M...... Iloilo.	Clark, Jesse W	Captain	Commanding company
	French W. Harry.......	1st Lieutenant.....	With company
	Logan, Guy E	2d Lieutenant	" "

Twentieth Regiment Kansas Volunteer Infantry.

COMPANIES AND ADDRESS.	OFFICERS.	RANK.	DUTY.
Headquarters	Funston, Frederick ...	Colonel.	Commanding regiment
Field. Staff, and	Little. Edward C. ..	Lieut. Colonel	Commanding 1st battalion
Band	Whitman, Frank H....	Major	Commanding 2d battalion
Administracion de	Metcalf, Wilder S.......	Major....	Commanding 3d battalion
Hacienda.	Rafter, John A.........	Major and Surgeon...	With regiment
	Huffman, Charles S.....	Captain and A. S....	" 18th Infantry, Iloilo
	Smith, Henry D....	Captain and A. S....	" regiment
	Schlieman, John G......	Captain and Chap.	" "
	Walker, Charles B......	1st. Lieut. and Adj..	" "
	Hull, Walter P....... ...	1st. Lieut. and Q. M.	" "
Company A.....	Towers, John E........	Captain............	On D. S. at San Francisco
La Rosa Tobaco	Frank, Frank J...	1st Lieutenant....	Commanding company
Warehouse.	Huddleston, Everett E...	2d Lieutenant.......	With company
Company B. ...	Buchan, Fred E..	Captain............	A. A. G., 1st Brigade, 2d Division
La Rosa Tobaco	Alford, Alfred C	1st Lieutenant......	Commanding company
Warehouse.	Showalter, Edwin B..	2d Lieutenant.......	With company
Company C.....	Albright, William S.....	Captain	Commanding company
Aldecoa & Co's	Seckler, Harry H......	1st Lieutenant......	With company
Godown.	Hauserman, John W....	2d Lieutenant.......	Regimental Commissary
Company D.....	Oxwig, Henry B........	Captain..........	Commanding company
Aldecoa & Co's	Watson, William J......	1st Lieutenant......	With company
Godown.	Burton, Orlando J..	2d Lieutenant.......	" "
Company E.....	Christy, Charles M.....	Captain...........	Commanding company
Administracion de	Craig, Daniel F........	1st Lieutenant......	With company
Hacienda.	Ball, Colton H.........	2d Lieutenant.......	" "
Company F. ...	Martin, Charles E	Captain.........	Commanding company
La Rosa Tobaco	Green, William A	1st Lieutenant....	With company
Warehouse.	Shideler, Harry W.....	2d Lieutenant.	" "
Company G. ...	Elliott, David S	Captain........	Commanding company
Administracion de	Scott. Howard A..	1st Lieutenant..t....	Regimental ordnance officer
Hacienda.	McTaggart, William A...	2d Lieutenant.	With company
Company H.	Clark, Adna G.........	Captain.........	Commanding company
Aldecoa & Co's	Krause, Albert H......	1st Lieutenant......	With company
Godown.	Hardy, Edward C ..	2d Lieutenant.......	" "
Company I..	Flanders, Charles S.....	Captain...........	Commanding company
Aldecoa & Co s	Agnew, Ernest J.......	1st Lieutenant	With company
Godown.	Dodge, Frederick R. .	2d Lieutenant.......	" "
Company K....	Boltwood, Edmond	Captain...	Commanding company
Administracion de	Hall, John F.	1st Lieutenant	With company
Hacienda.	Parker, Robert S.......	2d Lieutenant......	" "
Company L.. ..	Watson, George N.....	Captain.	Commanding company
La Rosa Tobaco	Fry, Edgar A....	1st Lieutenant	With company
Warehouse.	Callahan, William A....	2d Lieutenant.......	" "
Company M....	Bishop. William H......	Captain.........	Commanding company
Administracion de	Glasgow, Edward L.....	1st Lieutenant	With company
Hacienda.	Hamilton, Clad	2d Lieutenant......	" "

Thirteenth Regiment Minnesota Volunteer Infantry.

COMPANIES AND ADDRESS.	OFFICERS.	RANK.	DUTY.
Headquarters Field, Staff and Band. Suspension bridge, west end.	Ames, Frederick W	Colonel	Commanding regiment
	Friedrich, John H	Lieut. Colonel	On leave
	Bean, Edwin S.	Major	Charge Bilibid Prison. Man.
	Diggles, Arthur M	Major	Cm'd'g. 1st bat. and Inspector of Military Police
	Fitz Gerald, Reynaldo J.	Major and Surgeon.	1st Reserve Hospital
	Law, Arthur A	Captain and A. S.	With regiment
	Ritchie, Harry P	1st Lieut. and A. S.	With regiment
	Cressy, Charles A	Captain and Chap.	" "
	Faulk, Edward G	1st Lieut. and Adj't.	" "
	Hart, Wm. H	1st Lieut. and Q. M.	" "
	Conrad, Edwin M.	1st Lieut., Bat. Adj.	" "
	Garcelon, Monroe D	1st Lieut., Bat. Adj.	Aide-de-Camp, to Brigadier General Reeves.
	Mead, Milton S	1st Lieut., Bat. Adj.	Sick in Hospital
Company A. Paco, near cemetery	McWade, Wm. S	Captain	Sick in quarters
	Pearse, Roy	1st Lieutenant	Commanding company
	Donaldson, John	2d Lieutenant	Q. M. and Com. of Regimental Hospital.
Company B. Cor. Bustillos and Manrique. Sampaloc	Rowley, Frank B	Captain	Commanding company
	Keiler, Harry L	1st Lieutenant	With company
	Fitzgerald, Don F	2d Lieutenant	Sick in hospital
Company C Lemeri, (near Pasco) Tondo.	Robinson, Noyes C	Captain	Comdg company, and 3d bat.
	Bunker, Clarence G	1st Lieutenant	On leave
	Snow, James F	2d Lieutenant	With company
Company D. San Fernands and Numantia, Binondo.	Metz, Charles E.	Captain	Commanding company
	Merrill, Milford L	1st Lieutenant	On duty at Bilibid Prison. Manila
	Tenvoorde, Henry W	2d Lieutenant	With company
Company E. Intramuros, Cabildo.	Spear, Charles T	Captain	Commanding company
	Clark, Charles A	1st Lieutenant	Aide-de-Camp to Brig. Gen. R. P. Hughes
	Trowbridge, Charles. R.	2d Lieutenant	With company
Company F. 37 Novaliches, San Miguel.	Carleton, William A	Captain	Commanding company
	Clark, Charles N	1st Lieutenant	With company
	Stone, Carl L	2d Lieutenant	" "
Company G Intramuros, St Thomas.	Seebach, Oscar	Captain	Commanding company
	Mellinger, Edward S	1st Lieutenant	With company
	Anderson, Carl A	2d Lieutenant	" "
Company H Quiapo.	Bjornstad, Alfred W	Captain	Commanding company
	Sauter, Frank C	1st Lieutenant	With company
	Whitney, David H	2d Lieutenant	" "
Company I No. 1 Elizondo, Quipo.	Corriston, Frank T	Captain	Commanding company
	Byrnes, William J	1st Lieutenant	With company
	Chambers, John F	2d Lieutenant	" "
Company K. Intramuros, Palace of Civil Governor.	Masterman, Joseph P	Captain	Com'dg. company and 2d bat. Inspector of Milt'y. Police.
	Walsh, John J	1st Lieutenant	With company
	Grant, George H	2d Lieutenant	" "
Company L. Dolores, Santa Cruz.	Morgan, Alfred S	Captain	Commanding company
	Lackore, Harry D	1st Lieutenant	On duty in office of Provost Marshal General
	Scott, Hugh R	2d Lieutenant	With company
Company M 19 Calle Real, Intramuros.	McKelvey, Joseph E	Captain	Commanding company
	Bruckart, Leigh D	1st Lieutenant	With company
	Limperich, Henry J	2d Lieutenant	Sick in quarters.

First Regiment Montana Volunteer Infantry.

COMPANIES AND ADDRESS.	OFFICERS.	RANK.	DUTY.
Headquarters	Kessler, Harry C........	Colonel............	Commanding regiment
Field Staff and	Wallace, Robert B....	Lieut. Colonel......	With regiment
Band	Drennan, James W	Major.............	Commanding 1st battalion
	Cook, Byron H........	Major.............	Commanding 2d battalion
No. 23, San Miguel	Miller, John R.........	Major	Commanding 3d battalion
	Adams, Francis J......	Major and Surgeon..	With regiment
	Southmayd, Leroy.....	1st Lieut. and A. S.	Duty 2d Reserve Hospital
	Bruning, Lou C........	1st Lieut. and A. S.	With regiment
	Stull, George C........	Captain and Chap...	" "
	Calkins, Benjamin E....	1st Lieut. and Adj't.	On leave
	Seadorf, Alfred........	1st Lieut. and Q. M.	With regiment............
	Sanders, Louis P.......	1st Lieut. & Bat.Adjt	Aid-de-Camp to Major Gen. Otis.
	Hanna, William B.	1st Lieut. & Bat. Adjt	Duty with company
	Brown, William........	1st Lieut. & Bat. Adjt	Duty with company M
Company A......	Moran, John E,.......	Captain	Commanding company
No. 23, San Miguel	French, Charles, ...	1st Lieutenant......	With company
	Boardman, Clarence I...	2d Lieutenant	" "
Company B......	Gardner, Charles.... ...	Captain	Commanding company
No. 23, San Miguel	McGrath, William F....	1st Lieutenant......	With company
	Corby, Joseph	2d Lieutenant.....	" "
Company C.....	Keown, James F........	Captain	Commanding company
No. 12, San Miguel	Mercer, John F.........	1st Lieutenant......	With company
	Poorman, William H....	2d Lieutenant	" "
Company D....	Reif, George W.........	Captain	Commanding company
No. 23, San Miguel	Mead, Charles W......	1st Lieutenant......	With company
	Gainnan, Edward J.....	2d Lieutenant	" "
Company E... .	Jensen, Andrew........	Captain	Commanding company
No. 23, San Miguel	Bird, Fred J....	1st Lieutenant.....	With company
	Rickards, Homer L.....	2d Lieutenant	On duty with company M
Company F.....	Hill, William L....... ...	Captain	Commanding company
No. 23, San Miguel	Nickell, Gustav........	1st Lieutenant......	With company
	Keppner, Adolph.......	2d Lieutenant	" "
Company G.....	Wynne, Ellis W........	Captain	Commanding company
No. 23, San Miguel	Paxson, Edgar S	1st Lieutenant	On leave
	Knowlton, William B ..	1st Lieutenant......	Acting Regimental Adjutant
	(vacancy).............	2d Lieutenant	....
Company H. ...	Green, Frank E........	Captain	Commanding company
No. 12, Guano St	Hilburn, Samuel	1st Lieutenant......	With company
	McIntyre, Byron J......	2d Lieutenant	" "
Company I.....	Preston, Guy H........	Captain	Commanding company
No. 23, San Miguel	Foster, Edward A......	1st Lieutenant.	With company
	Croft, James F.	2d Lieutenant	In charge of post exchange
Company K....	Dillon, Thomas S......	Captain	Commanding company
No. 12, Guana St..	Kennedy, Jacob M......	1st Lieutenant	With company
	Greenan, Philip.......	2d Lieutenant	" "
Company L......	Duncan, Asa L........	Captain	Commanding company
No. 12, Guano St	Bradshaw, Walter J.....	1st Lieutenant	With company
	French, Eugene S.......	2d Lieutenant	" "
Company M.....	Hallahan, John.........	Captain	Commanding company
No. 23, San Miguel	(vacancy)..	1st Lieutenant......	....
	Sullivan, Gerald..	2d Lieutenant	On duty with company E

First Regiment Nebraska Volunteer Infantry.

COMPANIES AND ADDRESS.	OFFICERS.	RANK.	DUTY.
Headquarters Field Staff and Band........ Camp Santa Mesa	Stotsenburg, John M....	Colonel............	Commanding regiment
	Colton, Geo. R.........	Lieut. Colonel......	Collector of Customs
	Mulford, Harry B.....	Major..........	Commanding battalion
	Snyder, Frank A........	Major and Surgeon..	With regiment
	Mullins, Chas. L........	Captain and A. S....	Charge of sick on S S Ohio, en route to U. S.
	Jensen, Robert P.......	1st Lieut. and A. S.	With regiment
	Mailley, James..........	Captain. and Chap...	" "
	Forby, Lee	1st Lieut. and Adj't.	" "
	McLaughlin, Warren R..	1st Lieut. and Q. M.	" "
Company A...... Camp Santa Mesa	Holdeman, Geo. H.. ..	Captain	Commanding company
	Yale, Fred M...........	1st Lieutenant	With company
	Corcoran, Daniel......	2d Lieutenant	" "
Company B..... Camp Santa Mesa	Ough, Claude H........	Captain........	Commanding company
	Smith, John T.........	1st Lieutenant.... .	With company
	Storch, Joseph A......	2d Lieutenant	" "
Company C... .. Camp Santa Mesa	Hollingworth, Albert H.	Captain	Commanding company
	Archer, Harry L........	1st Lieutenant......	With company
	Whedon, Bert D	2d Lieutenant	On leave
Company D..... Camp Santa Mesa	Herpolsheimer, Martin..	Captain	Commanding company
	Cosgrave. P. James.....	1st Lieutenant......	With company
	Russell, Philip P........	2d Lieutenant	Aid to Brig. Gen'l H. G. Otis
Company E..... Camp Santa Mesa	Zeilinger, John F......	Captain	Commanding company
	Naracong, Frank B.....	1st Lieutenant......	With company
	White, Sherman A......	2d Lieutenant	" "
Company F.... Camp Santa Mesa	Vickers, Charles A......	Captain	On leave
	Gegner, Fred...	1st Lieutenant......	Commanding company
	Henderson, Jacob.......	2d Lieutenant	With company
Company G...... Camp Santa Mesa	Williams, Fred A.......	Captain	Commanding company
	Burr, George W........	1st Lieutenant... ...	With company
	Fisher, Burton.........	2d Lieutenant......	" "
Company H..... Camp Santa Mesa	Eagar, Frank D.	Captain	Commanding company
	Moore, William K.......	1st Lieutenant......	With company
	Van Valin, Alexander...	2d Lieutenant	" "
Company I...... Camp Santa Mesa	Stockham, Wm. E......	Captain	Commanding company
	Hansén, Christian	1st Lieutenant......	With company
	Smith, Andrew I.'......	2d Lieutenant	" "
Company K...... Camp Santa Mesa	Killan, Julius W........	Captain	Commanding company
	Jens, Chas. W.........	1st Lieutenant......	With company
	Webber, Ernest O.	2d Lieutenant	" "
Company L...... Camp Santa Mesa	Taylor, Wallace C.......	Captain	Commanding company
	Richards, Charles M.....	1st Lieutenant.......	With company
	Thomsett, Jesse M......	2d Lieutenant	" "
Company M..... Camp Santa Mesa	Wilson, Lincoln..........	Captain	Commanding company
	Talbot, V. Claris........	1st Lieutenant	With company
	Orr, Charles T.........	2d Lieutenant	" "

First Regiment North Dakota Volunteer Infantry.

COMPANIES AND ADDRESS.	OFFICERS	RANK.	DUTY.
Headquarters	Treumann, Wm. C...	Lieut. Colonel.....	Commanding regiment
Field, Staff and	White, Frank.......	Major.............	Commanding 1st battalion
Band ...	Fraine, John H......	Major.............	Commanding 2d battalion
No. 92 Calle Real,	Pease, Frank D........	Major and Surgeon..	With regiment
Ermita.	Black, Nelson M	Captain and A. S....	1st Reserve hospital
	Procter, Herbert J	1st Lieut. and Adjt..	With regiment
	Berg, Ingerwald A	1st Lieut. and Q. M..	" "
Company A ...	Moffet, Wm. P.........	Captain	In charge of records of prisons of Manila.
Opp. Cuartel de Malate.	Newcomer, Sherman H..	1st Lieutenant......	Commanding company
	McLean, Wm. J........	2d Lieutenant......	With company
Company B..	Keye, Frederick........	Captain	On leave
Near Fort San	Gearey, Edward C. Jr.	1st Lieutenant.....	Commanding company
Antonio, Malate.	Hildreth, Melvin A....	2d Lieutenant	With company
Company C ...	Johnson, John H	Captain...........	Commanding company
Opp. Cuartel de	Foley, Cornelius J	1st Lieutenant.....	With company
Malate.	Tharalson, Thos. H	2d Lieutenant .	" "
Company D	Cogswell, Adelbert W...	Captain	Commanding company
Opp. Cuartel de	Redmon, Henry........	1st Lieutenant	With company
Malate.	Lonnevik, Thomas	2d Lieutenant .	" "
Company G	Mudgett, Chas. F,.....	Captain	Collector of Internal Revenue
No. 202 Calle Nueva	Getchell, Chas. W......	1st Lieutenant...	Commanding company
de Malate.	Pray, Wm. H	2d Lieutenant......	With company
Company H......	Eddy, Porter W	Captain...........	Commanding company
Opp. Cuartel de	Conklin, Fred L......	1st Lieutenant......	On leave
Malate.	Baldwin, Dorman, Jr....	2d Lieutenant	Battalion Adjutant.
Company I.	Purdon, Wm. M........	Captain	Commanding company
Opp. Cuartel de	Aspinwall, Wm. B......	1st Lieutenant	With company
Malate.	Slattery, Jos. H........	2d Lieutenant	" "
Company K. ...	Auld, George.	Captain	Commanding company
Opp. Cuartel de	Osborn, Ambrose J....	1st Lieutenant	Battalion Adj't.
Malate.	Gruschus, Harry J....	2d Lieutenant	With company

Second Regiment Oregon Volunteer Infantry.

COMPANIES AND ADDRESS.	OFFICERS.	RANK.	DUTY.
Headquarters Field. Staff and Band. Cuartel Espana.	Summers, Owen	Colonel	Commanding regiment
	Yoran, Geo. O	Lieut. Colonel	With regiment
	Gantenbein, C. U.	Major	Commanding 1st battalion
	Willis, Percy	Major	Commanding 2d battalion
	Eastwick, P. G. Jr	Major	Commanding 3d battalion
	Ellis, M. H	Major, Surgeon	With regiment
	Whiting, Sanford	Capt. and Asst. Surg	On duty in Small-pox Hosp
	Gilbert, Wm. S	Captain and Chap.	With regiment
	Crowne, E. P	1st Lieut. and Adj't.	" "
	Knapp, L. H	1st Lieut. and Q. M.	" "
Company A Cuartel Espana.	Heath. H. L	Captain	Commanding company
	Platt, Ralph	1st Lieutenant	A. J. A., Provost Marshal General's Hdqrs.
	Young. J. A	2d Lieutenant	With company
Company B Cuartel Espana.	May, J. L	Captain	Commanding company
	Hamlin, F. B	1st Lieutenant	With company
	Thornton, J. E	2d Lieutenant	Sick in quarters
Company C Cuartel Espana.	Moon, W. S	Captain	Commanding company
	Huston, R. S	1st Lieutenant	With company
	Haynes, F. W	2d Lieutenant	Acting Ordnance Officer
Company D Cuartel Espana.	Prescott, A. F	Captain	Commanding company
	Hartman, Geo. A. Jr	1st Lieutenant	With company
	Kelly, F. S	1st Lieutenant	On duty with Company A
	Meade, F. A	2d Lieutenant	With company
Company E Cuartel Espana.	Davis, R. E	Captain	Sick in quarters
	Dunbar, T. N	1st Lieutenant	Commanding company
	Brazee, A. J	1st Lieutenant	Adj. 2d bat., Sick in Hosp.
	Bryan, E. J	2d Lieutenant	On leave
Company F Ayuntamiento, Old Manila.	Case, J. F	Captain	Commanding company
	Grimm, Edwin	1st Lieutenant	With company
	Jackson, Rheese	1st Lieutenant	Adjutant 3d battalion
	(vacancy)	2d Lieutenant	
Company G Cuartel Espana.	Gadsby, Wm	Captain	On leave
	Barber, R. H	1st Lieutenant	Commanding company
	Wolfe, Geo. N	2d Lieutenant	Duty at Presidio de Manila
Company H Custom House.	McDonald, C. E	Captain	Commanding company
	Gritzmacher, A. B	1st Lieutenant	With company
	McKinnon, J. A	2d Lieutenant	" "
Company I Cuartel Espana.	Pickens, L. L	Captain	Commanding company
	Phillips, M. D	1st Lieutenant	With company
	Huntley, W. A	2d Lieutenant	On leave
Company K Cuartel Espana.	Warrick, E. O	Captain	Commanding company
	Terrell, Ralph	1st Lieutenant	With company
	Murphy, Chas. A	2d Lieutenant	On duty with Company F
Company L Cuartel Espana.	Wells, H. L	Captain	Commanding company
	Telfer, Geo. F	1st Lieutenant	With company
	Povey, Geo. W	2d Lieutenant	Depot Q. M., Cavite
Company M Cuartel Espana.	Poorman, J. M	Captain	Sick in quarters
	Finzer, W. E	1st Lieutenant	Commanding company
	Platts, C. R	2d Lieutenant	Sick in quarters

Tenth Regiment Pennsylvania Volunteer Infantry.

COMPANIES AND ADDRESS.	OFFICERS.	RANK.	DUTY.
Headquarters	Hawkins, Alexander L	Colonel	Commanding regiment
Field Staff and	Barnett, James E	Lieut. Colonel	Commanding Det. of 1st Bat
Band	Cuthburtson, Harry C	Major	Commanding companies A & B, at Corregidor Island
Parque de Bombe-	Bierer, Everhart	Major	Commanding Det. of 2d Bat.
ros, Santa Cruz,	Neff, George W	Major and Surgeon	With regiment
cor. Alcala and	Coffin, John J	1st Lieut. and A. S.	" "
Enrile Streets.	McCormick, Lewis P	1st Lieut. and A. S.	Duty, 1st Reserve Hospital
	Hunter, Joseph I	Captain and Chaplain	With regiment
	Duncan, Harry B	1st Lieut. and Adjt.	On D. S. to U. S.
	McCormick, Edward B	1st Lieut. and Q. M.	On D. S. to U. S.
	Scott, Oliver S	2d Lieutenant	Acting Adjutant
Company A	Schaaf, Gustav	Captain	Commanding company
Corregidor Island,	Tidball, Robert T	1st Lieutenant	With company
Manila Bay.	Ewing, John A	2d Lieutenant	" "
Company B	Watson, Harry J	Captain	Commanding company
Corregidor Island,	Carey, Edwin H	1st Lieutenant	With company
Manila Bay.	Thomas, Elmer H	2d Lieutenant	" "
Company C	Bierer, Daniel M	Captain	Commanding company
No. 44, Calle de	Howard, Charles H	1st Lieutenant	With company
Iris.	Wood, Robert M	2d Lieutenant	" "
Company D	Hawkins, Frank B	Captain	Commanding company
No. 22 Calle, de	Crow, Husted A	1st Lieutenant	With company
Iris.	Buttermore, Albert J	2d Lieutenant	" "
Company E	Loar, James A	Captain	Commanding company
Mountain of Piety	Harkins, James	1st Lieutenant	Acting Quartermaster of Reg.
Bank Santa Cruz	Thompson, John G	2d Lieutenant	With company
Plaza, at opening			
of Escolta.			
Company H	Porter, Alonzo M	Captain	Commanding company
No. 42, Calle de	Aiken, Blaine	1st Lieutenant	With company
Iris.	Ritchie, William B	2d Lieutenant	" "
Company I	Finney, William S	Captain	Commanding company
No. 42, Calle de	Laird, Richard D	1st Lieutenant	With company
Iris.	Coulter, Richard Jr.	2d Lieutenant	" "
Company K	Crago, Thomas S	Captain	Commanding company
No. 22, Calle de	Wiley, John M	1st Lieutenant	On leave
Iris.	Gordon, George L	2d Lieutenant	With company

First Regiment South Dakota Volunteer Infantry.

COMPANIES AND ADDRESS.	OFFICERS.	RANK.	DUTY.
Headquarters **Field Staff** **and Band.** No. 10, Malacanan.	Frost, Alfred S. Stover, Lee Howard, Charles A. Allison, William F. Warne, Rodell C Bowman, Adelbert H Cox, Frederick W Daley, Charles M Lien, Jonas H. Murray, Henry	Colonel Lieut. Colonel Major Major Major and Surgeon Captain and A. S. Captain and A. S. Captain and Chaplain 1st Lieut. and Adj't 1st Lieut. and Q. M	Commanding regiment Sick in quarters Commanding 2d battalion Commanding 3d battalion With regiment " " " " " " " " " "
Company A. No. 1, Concepcion.	Fuller, Arthur L. Harting, Edwin A Guthrie, Munson M. Z.	Captain. 1st Lieutenant. 2d Lieutenant.	Commanding company Acting commissary of reg't With company
Company B No. 2, Malacanan.	Sessions, Alonzo B. Fox, John C. Hawkins, Edwin E	Captain 1st Lieutenant 2d Lieutenant	Commanding company Adj't. 1st battalion With company
Company C No. 1, Concepcion.	Gray, William S. Foster, Leo. F Larson, Samuel G	Captain 1st Lieutenant 2d Lieutenant	Commanding company Sick in quarters With company
Company D. No. 10, Malacanan	Van Houten, Clayton P. Dynna, Ludwig L. Jennings, George G.	Captain 1st Lieutenant. 2d Lieutenant	Commanding company With company Postmaster at Cavite
Company E No. 10, Malacanan.	Lattin, George W Hubbard, J. Harris. Morrison, Sidney E.	Captain 1st Lieutenant 2d Lieutenant	Commanding company With company " "
Company F. No. 10, Malacanan	Brockway, Charles L. Sheldon, Palmer D. Huntington, Fred G.	Captain 1st Lieutenant 2d Lieutenant	Commanding company Adjutant 2d battalion Sick in quarters
Company G. No. 5, Concepcion.	McGregor, Robert R. Fisk, Olin M. Hazle, William A.	Captain 1st Lieutenant 2d Lieutenant	Commanding company Adjutant 3d battalion With company
Company H. No. 2, Malacanan.	Englesby, Charles H. Adams, Frank H Mowrey, Harry J	Captain 1st Lieutenant 2d Lieutenant	Commanding company and 1st battalion With company " "
Company I No. 2, Malacanan.	Denny, Charles S. McClelland, Paul D. Bates, Horace C	Captain 1st Lieutenant 2d Lieutenant	On leave Commanding company With company
Company K. No. 2, Malacanan.	Hegeman, Harry A Roskie, George W Smith, Oscar F	Captain 1st Lieutenant 2d Lieutenant	Commanding company With company " "
Company L. No. 5, Concepcion.	McLaughlin, William Braden, John Q. A Crabtree, George H	Captain 1st Lieutenant 2d Lieutenant	Commanding company Sick in quarters With company
Company M. No. 10, Malacanan	Medbery, Frank W Burdick, Fred L Young, Evan E	Captain 1st Lieutenant 2d Lieutenant	Commanding company With company " "

First Regiment Tennessee Volunteer Infantry.

COMPANIES AND ADDRESS.	OFFICERS.	RANK.	DUTY.
Headquarters	Smith, William C.	Colonel	Com'd'g. Reg.& Dis.of Cavite
Field, Staff and	Childers, Gracey	Lieut. Colonel	Com'd'g. 1st and 3d battalions
Band	Bayless, Albert B	Major	Commanding 1st battalion
Cavite Arsenal.	Cheatham, B. Frank	Major	Commanding 2d battalion
	McGuire, John G.	Major	Commanding 3d battalion
	Barr, Richard A.	Major and Surgeon	With regiment
	Kirby-Smith, R. M.	Captain and A. S.	" "
	Jones, Percy L.	Captain and A. S.	" "
	Leland, Lewis J.	Captain and Chap.	" "
	Polk, James K.	1st Lieut. and Adj.	" "
	Duncan, Andrew J.	1st Lieut. and Q. M.	Sick in San Francisco
Company A.	Reed, George.	Captain	Commanding company
Camp Hughes, west	Alexander, William A.	1st Lieutenant	With company
of Walled City.	McLester, Charles M	2d Lieutenant	" "
Company B.	Whitthorne, William J.	Captain	Commanding company
Cuartel de Infanteria	Ragsdale, Robert O.	1st Lieutenant.	With company
de Marina, Cavite.	Baskette, Alvin K.	2d Lieutenant	" "
Company C	Richmond, Henry R.	Captain	Commanding company
Camp Hughes, west	Law, Alfred J.	1st Lieutenant	With company
of Walled City.	Martin, Robert E.	2d Lieutenant.	" "
Company D.	Gilbreath, William J	Captain	Commanding company
Fort San Felipe,	McNeal, Edward C.	1st Lieutenant	With company
Cavite.	Cocke, Joe B.	2d Lieutenant.	" "
Company E.	Hager, James F.	Captain	Commanding company
Camp Hughes, west	Chapman, Granville.	1st Lieutenant	With company
of Walled City.	Williams, S. Morgan	2d Lieutenant	" "
Company F.	Gillem, Alvan C.	Captain.	Commanding company
Camp Hughes, west	Milam, Robert M.	1st Lieutenant	With company
of Walled City.	Eastman, Henry N.	2d Lieutenant	" "
Company G.	Myers, H. B.	Captain	Commanding company
Camp Hughes, west	Sarkman, Hugh.	1st Lieutenant	With company
of Walled City.	Bates, Thomas F.	2d Lieutenant.	" "
Company H.	O'Brien, Gaston.	Captain.	Commanding company
Camp Hughes, west	Johnson, Cave.	1st Lieutenant	With company
of Walled City.	Stacker, Pat L.	2d Lieutenant.	Acting Regimental Q. M.
Company I	Givens, Nick K.	Captain.	Commanding company
Camp Hughes, west	Caraway, Leon.	1st Lieutenant	With company
of Walled City.	Bowles, Ernest B.	2d Lieutenant	" "
Company K.	Murphy, Sam O.	Captain.	Commanding company
Camp Hughes, west	Patton, John C.	1st Lieutenant	With company
of Walled City.	Pickard, Nixon N.	2d Lieutenant.	" "
Company L	Van Leer, Sam.	Captain	Commanding company
Fort San Felipe,	Van Leer, Carlos	1st Lieutenant	With company, Ord. Officer
Cavite.	Pilcher, Winston	2d Lieutenant.	With company
Company M	Clark, Sheffield.	Captain.	Commanding company
Cuartel de Infanteria	Bright, Albert J	1st Lieutenant.	With company
de Marina, Cavite.	Dismukes, Martin	2d Lieutenant.	On leave

First Regiment Washington Volunteer Infantry.

COMPANIES AND ADDRESS.	OFFICERS.	RANK.	DUTY.
Headquarters Field, Staff and Band No. 73 Calle Nozalado, Paco.	Wholley, John H	Colonel	Commanding regiment
	Fife, William J	Lieut. Colonel	In arrest
	Weisenburger, John J.	Major	Commanding 1st battalion
	Dawson, Lewis R	Major and Surgeon.	With regiment
	Van Patten, William Mc.	1st Lieut. and A. S.	" "
	Brown, Elmer M	1st Lieut. and A. S.	" "
	Thompson, John R.	Captain and Chap.	" "
	Luhn, William L	1st Lieut. and Adj.	" "
	Bryan, Albert W	1st Lieut. and Q. M.	" "
Company A Tobaco Fabrica, Paco.	Otis, Albert H	Captain	Commanding company
	Erwin, Edward K	1st Lieutenant	With company
	Hinckley, William J	2d Lieutenant	At Presidio San Francisco
Company B. Tobaco Fabrica, Paco.	Fortson, George H	Captain	Commanding company
	Gormley, Matt. H	1st Lieutenant	With company
	Moss, Harvey J	2d Lieutenant	Regt'l Signal Officer
Company C No. 7 Calle LePaz, Paco.	Sturges, Edward A	Captain	Commanding company
	Bothwell, Samuel C	1st Lieutenant	With company
	McCoy, John B	2d Lieutenant	" "
Company D. Tobaco Fabrica, Paco.	Adams, Frank E	Captain	Commanding company
	Egell, Henry L	1st Lieutenant	With company
	Lamping, George B	2d Lieutenant	" "
Company E. Tobaco Fabrica, Paco.	Scudder, Marshall S	Captain	Commanding company
	Briggs, Fred T	1st Lieutenant	With company
	Lemon, William T	2d Lieutenant	A. A. C. S. and A. A. Q. M.
Company F. Bishop's Palace, Calle Nozalada, Paco.	Miller, Chester F	Captain	Commanding company
	Booker, Charles A	1st Lieutenant	With company
	Dorr, George B	2d Lieutenant	" "
Company G. Bishop's Palace, Calle Nozalada, Paco.	Ellrich, Max F	Captain	In arrest
	Weigle, William E	1st Lieutenant	Commanding company
	(Vacancy)	2d Lieutenant	
Company H No. 7 Calle LePaz, Paco.	Steinman, Alfred C	Captain	Commanding company
	Southern, Edward E	1st Lieutenant	With company
	Smith, Joe	2d Lieutenant	" "
Company I Bishop's Palace, Calle Nozalada, Paco.	Buffum, William B	Captain	Sick in quarters
	Gustin, Morrow C	1st Lieutenant	Commanding company
	Hart, Thomas D. S	2d Lieutenant	Sick in quarters
Company K No. 3 San Marcelino, Paco.	Smith, Charles T	Captain	Commanding company
	Arnold, Jesse H	1st Lieutenant	With company
	Caldwell, John B	2d Lieutenant	" "
Company L Bishop's Palace, Calle Nozalada, Paco.	Moore, Joseph M	Captain	Commanding company
	Ballaine, John E	1st Lieutenant	With company
	Nosler, Charles E	2d Lieutenant	" "
Company M No. 3 San Marceline, Paco.	Boyer, John E	Captain	Sick in San Francisco
	Dreher, George M	1st Lieutenant	Commanding company
	Hazzard, Russell T	2d Lieutenant	With company

First Battalion Wyoming Volunteer Infantry.

COMPANIES AND ADDRESS.	OFFICERS.	RANK.	DUTY.
Headquarters Calle Arsenal, Cavite.	Foote, Frank M	Major	Commanding battalion
	Morrison, John E	1st Lieut. and A. S.	With battalion
Company C Church "Recollecta," Cavite.	Millar, Thomas	Captain	Commanding company
	Gallup, James D	1st Lieutenant	Battalion Adjutant
	Cheever, Loren	2d Lieutenant	With company
Company F Calle Arsenal, Cavite.	O'Brien, John D	Captain	Commanding company
	Coburn, Harold D	1st Lieutenant	With company
	Rouse, Willard H	2d Lieutenant	" "
Company G Calle Novaleiches, Cavite.	Wrighter, Daniel C	Captain	Commanding company
	Howe, Hezekiah P	1st Lieutenant	With company
	Morgareidge, J. W	2d Lieutenant	Acting Quartermaster
Company H Church "Recollecta," Cavite.	Holtenhouse, Edward P	Captain	Commanding company
	Ohlenkamp, Henry	1st Lieutenant	With company
	Fast, George F	2d Lieutenant	Battalion, Q. M., (sick)

DIRECTORY

— OF

GENERAL AND STAFF OFFICERS.

No. 16 Calle Gral Solano.. Mallory, J. S............No. 16 Calle Gral Solano
No. 2 Calle Real In-
  tramuros...........Martin C. H.............No. 6 Calle Real, Malate
Ayuntamiento........McClure, Chas............No: 94 Calle Real, Malate
...................Miller, M. P............................Iloilo
Administration Building,
  Cavite.......Milliken, Seth M................Cavite Arsenal
Ayuntamiento.....Murray, C. H...............Malacanan Palace
Ayuntamiento.......Otis, E. S...............Malacanan Palace
No. 1-3 Calle Santa Mesa. Otis, H. G........No. 1-3 Calle Santa Mesa
No. 80 Calle Real Malate. Ovenshine, Sam'l.........No. 80 Calle Real, Malate
...................Perry, A W....................Iloilo
Ayuntamiento.......Pope, J. W....No. 94 Calle Real, Malate
Ayuntamiento.......Potter, C. L............No. 110 Calle Real, Malate
Corner Calle Real and
  Magellanes.......Reeve, C. McC...........No. 88 Calle Real, Ermita
Ayuntamiento........Rochester, W. B., Jr......No. 6 Calle Real, Malate
Ayuntamiento......Sanders, L. P..............Malacanan Palace
No. 16 Calle Gral Solano. Sawtelle, C. G...........No. 16 Calle Gral Solano
Casa Arellano Calle Real,
  Malate...Saxton, S. S..... Casa Arellano Calle Real, Malate
Ayuntamiento..Schofield, W. B..........No. 8 San Jose, Ermita
Ayuntamiento..Sears, J. M...................No. 44 Calle Marina
Ayuntamiento.. Sheary, M. F............No. 41 Calle Real, Ermita
Ayuntamiento..Sladen, F. W...............Malacanan Palace
Ayuntamiento.......Sternberg, T........................English Hotel
No. 16 Calle Gral Solano. Strong, P. B.............No. 16 Calle Gral Solano
Ayuntamiento....Sulzer, R...........No. 34 Calle Alix, Sampaloc
Ayuntamiento.......Thompson, R. E........No..101 Calle Real, Malate
No. 1-3 Calle Santa Mesa.. VanVoorhis, D...................On D. S. at Iloilo
No. 38 Calle Nozaleda,
  Paco.......Walcutt, C. C.............S. end Puente d'Ayala
    (No. 4 Concepcion)
Maestranza Arsenal. Wood, W. T.................Maestranza Arsenal

INDEX

Errors or omissions should be promptly reported to the Adjutant General, these headquarters.

THOMAS H. BARRY,
Assistant Adjutant General

HEADQUARTERS DEPARTMENT OF THE PACIFIC
AND EIGHTH ARMY CORPS,
Manila, P. I., January 1, 1899.

www.ingramcontent.com/pod-product-compliance
Lightning Source LLC
Chambersburg PA
CBHW030719110426
42739CB00030B/919